Practical
Pre-School Books

How children learn

by Linda Pound

Contents

Published by Practical Pre-School Books, A Division of MA Education Ltd,
St Jude's Church, Dulwich Road, London, SE24 0PB
Tel: 020 7738 5454
www.practicalpreschoolbooks.com

© MA Education Ltd 2006

Cover images from top to bottom © MARY EVANS PICTURE LIBRARY
(Johann Heinrich Pestalozzi; Friedrich Wilhelm August Froebel; Rudolph
Steiner; Dr Maria Montessori)

Illustrations by Cathy Hughes

ISBN: 978-1-90457-509-2

Introduction

This book is an attempt to explain educational and psychological theories about how children learn. It provides food for thought for reflective practitioners, encouraging you to pause and reconsider why you do what you do.

Theories can be rooted in research and experimentation or they may be philosophical and hypothetical. Whatever their basis, the importance of observation is a common strand in the work of many theorists who were interested in finding out how children learn.

Some were academics who became interested in children – others were experienced in working with children and developed theories to help them understand their experience. What is interesting is how often ideas which were based purely on observation are now supported by developmental theory.

We have singled out some of the key figures involved with theories about learning, particularly in the early years of education. In some cases these are linked to wider movements. Sigmund Freud, for example, is probably the best known psychoanalyst. However, other figures with psychoanalytical backgrounds who have perhaps had greater influence in education have also been included.

It is not clear why some names are remembered and others are not. Sigmund Freud is probably the best known psychoanalyst in this country, but in the United States Erikson and Fromm are more influential, perhaps because Freud fled from the Nazis to England, while Erikson and Fromm went to America. Howard Gardner (1) says that 'great psychologists put forward complex and intricate theories, but they are often remembered best for a striking demonstration. The founding behaviourist, Ivan Pavlov, showed that dogs can be conditioned to salivate at the sound of a bell. The founding psychoanalyst, Sigmund Freud, demonstrated that unconscious wishes - for example sexual satisfaction - are reflected in ordinary dreams or slips of the tongue. And Jean Piaget (1896-1980), the most important student of intellectual development, showed that young children are not able to conserve quantities, such as liquids.' This is something to think about as you read.

About this book

- To create a sense of the way in which ideas have developed and evolved, the theorists are taken in chronological order. Where a section focuses on an individual this is according to their date of birth. This does not work in every case – Piaget and Vygotsky, for example, were contemporaries but Vygotsky's work was not widely known until some time after his death.

Each section follows a similar format, beginning with some historical background and biographical details to place the person in context. Their theory is explained and the titles of any books or articles they have written are listed. There is also an attempt to link the theory with practice, and a 'Comment' encourages you to analyse any findings and perhaps apply them to your own experience .

You will find many strands and connections as you read as some theorists were influenced by the work of others. Margaret Donaldson, for example, spent time with Piaget and Bruner. Pestalozzi was influenced by Jean-Jacques Rousseau and in turn influenced Robert Owen and Froebel. Links with other theorists are highlighted.

Finally, some sections look at approaches rather than people that have been influential in the early years, such as High/Scope. Others cover the theory behind aspects such as emotional intelligence and play. We also offer an insight into the New Zealand curriculum, Te Whariki and an update on research into how the brain works.

Hopefully, this series of introductions will encourage you to delve deeper, helping you to understand and reflect on how you work with young children.

Reference
(1) Gardner *Intelligence: Multiple Perspectives* (Holt, Rinehart and Winston 1996) (page 97)

Note to students: Every effort has been made to make sure that you have the information you will need to cite sources in your essays and projects.

You will need to rearrange these references in your written work to meet the demands of your tutors. Double check before you hand in work that you have met the requirements of your place of study.

There is guidance in each section to help you track down further information for yourself. The information in this book is by no means the end of the story. There is much more to be read and learned from the remarkable figures outlined here. Many of the books mentioned are no longer in print, so check to see if your library can get a copy.

A word of caution about websites: some contain excellent information, others are worthless. Always think about who has published the information and why. Any website addresses provided were valid at the time of going to press.

John Comenius

1592 – 1670

His life

Jan Amos Komensky was born in Moravia in 1592, around the same time as the scientist, Galileo, the painter, Rembrandt and the writer, Milton. These three were significant figures at the beginning of a period known as the Age of Reason when thinking was characterised by people with inquiring minds who wanted evidence for arguments and often rejected traditional religious beliefs.

Comenius – as Komensky became known in a Latinised version of his name – was educated at the University of Heidelberg before becoming a bishop in the Moravian Church. It is thought that he was approached to become the first president of Harvard University, which was established in 1636, but declined because of the Church's troubles at that time.

In 1638 he was approached to restructure the Swedish school system – a role he took up in 1642. He was also invited to become a member of an English commission for the reform of education. Although he came to England, the Civil War made progress impossible and he left for Sweden.

At the end of the Thirty Years War, in 1648, Moravia became part of the Holy Roman Empire. Comenius led a small group of those who did not wish to join the Catholic Church into exile in Poland.

He died in Amsterdam in 1670 without seeing the Moravian Church re-established. After his death, however, his grandson became a bishop and presided over the renewal of the Church.

His writing

Comenius wrote more than 150 books, mostly on philosophy and theology. He wrote a novel called The Labyrinth of the World (1), which has been likened to John Bunyan's Pilgrim's Progress. In 1631, he published a book called The Gate of Tongues Unlocked which was designed to help children learn Latin through their first language. This was a significant shift from the normal approaches to learning Latin used at that time.

He developed this approach further with the publication, in 1658, of one of the first picture books for children, The Visible World in Pictures. It consisted of illustrations labelled in both Latin and the child's home language. It was translated into English in 1659.

His theory

Comenius believed that education begins in early childhood and should continue throughout life. He recommended sensory experiences rather than rote learning and was in favour of formal educational opportunities for women – an unusual idea in the seventeenth century.

He established a branch of philosophy that he called pansophism, which literally means 'all knowledge'. He believed that knowledge or learning, spirituality and emotional development were inseparable - a holistic view of education.

Putting the theory into practice

Comenius had high ideals and talked of developing schooling through play. There were few if any precursors to this in the seventeenth century. His emphasis on the senses was largely implemented through introducing illustrations to books. However, this was a radical step at the time.

His influence

Comenius' theories paved the way for subsequent developments in education. His understanding of the importance of learning through the senses and of the holistic nature of learning remain cornerstones of educational theories today.

Comment

Although Comenius' work was forward looking, it was a long way from what is now seen as learner-centred education. His idea of holistic education included the spiritual aspects of development and emotions but not physical development.

Reference
(1) This is available online on the Comenius Foundation website – www.comeniusfoundation.org/comenius.htm

Where to find out more
www.comeniusfoundation.org

Jean-Jacques Rousseau

PROFILE

Jean-Jacques Rousseau was a Swiss philosopher whose book, Emile, influenced child-rearing practices in eighteenth century France. Rousseau's educational theories continued to influence theorists and philosophers throughout the eighteenth and nineteenth centuries.

KEY DATES

1712	Born in Geneva, Switzerland
1724	Apprenticed to an engraver
1740	Becomes a tutor in Lyon
1745	Begins a relationship with Therese Levasseur
1762	*Emile* is published
1778	Dies in Ermenonville, France

LINKS

- Pestalozzi
- Froebel

His life

Jean-Jacques Rousseau's mother died when he was just a few days old and he was brought up by his father and an aunt.

At the age of 12 he was apprenticed to an engraver who treated him badly and when he was 16 he ran away. For the next ten years he travelled, staying in France and Italy. At 18, he decided to teach music, but gave up when he found he was only a little ahead of his pupils. His attempt to tutor two small boys in Lyon in 1740 lasted less than a year. It did, however, start him thinking about education.

In 1745, Rousseau began a relationship with Therese Levasseur, who was to bear him five children. All five were placed in an orphanage soon after their birth; it is said against their mother's wishes. It is also said that Rousseau came to regret this action later (1).

Rousseau wrote a number of books, but it was one called Emile that earned him a name in France. Parents claimed to be bringing up their children a la Jean-Jacques – which involved not having a wet nurse, being bathed in cold water and being flimsily dressed – to be closer to nature.

After his death, in 1778, crowds paid homage to him at his burial place.

His writing

Jean-Jacques Rousseau wrote a mixture of novels and non-fiction books on music, philosophy and politics. Emile – his book on education – is a mixture of fiction and philosophy. He also wrote a book called The Social Contract. (Both are published by Penguin.)

His theory

Rousseau described people as noble savages. He believed that we are born essentially good and are part of nature. Nature made children to be loved and helped but because they are innocent this help should not be intrusive. He wrote that adults should let children be children and revere childhood. He also believed in fostering self-reliance.

Rousseau thought that governments should work to establish freedom, equality and justice. Their role was not just to allow the will of the majority to hold sway but to take on the task of ensuring that everyone, including the weak, was protected.

Education would support this process by cultivating the good in people. We should all be educated for our own good, not for that of society which, Rousseau said, was corrupt.

Putting the theory into practice

Rousseau never put his theories into practice – he sent his own children to live in orphanages. However, many parents in eighteenth century France were influenced by Rousseau's writing. Until then, among members of French society it was accepted practice to place babies with wet nurses and swaddle them for their early months. This changed. Other writers and thinkers condemned these practices, but the changes were largely attributed to Rousseau.

Rousseau believed in freedom. He wrote, for example (4) that 'the only habit the child should be allowed is that of having no habits... Reverse the usual procedure and you will almost always do right'. While freedom included freedom from the swaddling clothes which restricted movement, it was also sometimes interpreted as letting children run about in light clothing even in bitter winter weather.

His influence

Rousseau highlighted the importance of observation. He said that teachers should 'take time to observe nature; watch your scholar well before you say a word to him; first leave the germ of his character free to show itself.'

While many of Rousseau's theories appear far fetched, he enabled people to think differently about the way in which children should be educated. His contribution to education perhaps has more to do with freeing up thinking, encouraging people to consider and try new ideas.

In 1788, after Rousseau's death, Madame de Stael, an eighteenth century writer and society figure, claimed that he 'had succeeded in restoring happiness to childhood' (5). Her support gave Rousseau's work some credibility.

In the same year, a critic in Paris wrote that in too many children 'hair straggles in a hideous and disgusting way... They are no longer checked but clamber on to you with their muddy feet. When you visit their parents they deafen you with their noise, and just when their father or mother is about to reply to you on some important matter, you see them choose instead to answer some childish question of their darling son or daughter..... It is Emile which is responsible for this provoking, obstinate, insolent, impudent, arrogant generation' (6).

Comment

The definitions which Rousseau uses in his writing make it difficult to follow exactly what he means. He says repeatedly, for example, that 'the first impulses of nature are always right' (2). However, he supports this claim by asserting that behaviour that is not inherently good cannot be natural. By this reasoning, any bad or evil actions are not part of nature.

His belief in the importance of freedom is supported by arguing that if a person does not feel constrained, then their liberty is not infringed. For Rousseau, 'Man feels free when he wants only what is within his reach' (3). In other words, self-discipline is the only true freedom.

The main criticism of his work is that his ideas were not practical and were open to misinterpretation.

References

(1) Rousseau, J-J Emile (Dent and Sons 1974). (These comments are in the introduction to this edition of Emile, which was written by P D Jimack.)
(2) See Jimack's introduction on page xviii
(3) See Jimack's introduction on page xix
(4) Jimack quotes these words from Emile on page xviii of his introduction
(5) Jimack quotes these words from Emile on page xxv of his introduction
(6) Jimack quotes these words from Emile on page xxv of his introduction

Where to find out more
Rousseau: A Very Short Introduction by R Wokler (Oxford University Press 2001)

Johann Pestalozzi

Pestalozzi was a Swiss educator whose ideas and practices laid the foundation for the reform of nineteenth century education. He put forward radical ideas that were later taken up and have now been absorbed into the way we educate young children.

KEY DATES

1746	Born in Zurich, Switzerland
1769	Marries Anna Schulthess
1770	Birth of son, named Jean-Jacques after Rousseau
1773	Opens experimental school
1781	Part one of Leonard and Gertrude is published
1799	Takes in war orphans at a school in Stans
1800	Directs educational establishment at Burgdorf
1801	How Gertrude Teaches her Children, the best known of Pestalozzi's books, is published
1805	Opens Yverdun Institute
1808	Works with Froebel
1818	Owen visits Yverdun
1827	Dies

LINKS

- Comenius
- Rousseau
- Owen
- Froebel

His life

Johann Heinrich Pestalozzi was born in Zurich, Switzerland in 1746, the second of three surviving children. His father, a surgeon, died when Pestalozzi was five, leaving his mother to bring them up with the help of the family servant. She had given her word before he died that she would stay with the family for as long as she was needed - and that was to be until her death 40 years later.

The children were severely restricted - not allowed out to play and rarely joined by other children. Johann went to school and learned easily, though he was often thought of as socially inept and teased by other children.

Interest in the poor

During his childhood, Pestalozzi would visit his grandfather at Hongg, a rural parish, and he became interested in the differences between country and townspeople. These experiences, together with the loyalty and devotion shown by his family's servant, developed his respect for the poor. He thought that children in the country seemed contented. He also noticed that once they started school it seemed as though they lost their vitality.

Pestalozzi went to elementary and grammar school, then the Collegium Humanitatis and finally the Collegium Carolinum where he studied philosophy and philology (the history and development of languages). He joined a historical-political organisation called The Patriots, who founded the Helvetic Society, a youth movement dedicated to raising moral standards. Members were expected to follow a life of self-denial and restraint and to show a strict sense of duty.

Pestalozzi grew tired of academic life and wanted to study farming. He met and fell in love with Anna Schulthess, and bought a house and some neglected land at Neuhof near the River Aare. In 1769 he married Anna. Five years later his farming enterprise failed.

Pestalozzi was still interested in the poor and helping the wider community and began taking children into his home, teaching them and setting them to work spinning, weaving, sewing and cooking. The idea was to teach the children to become self-supporting but it didn't work and, eventually, after five years, the children were sent away. Despite the failure, Pestalozzi still believed that his ideas for the education of the poor were practical and well-founded.

In 1770, Pestalozzi and his wife had a son, Jean-Jacques, named after Jean-Jacques Rousseau. He was a sickly child. Pestalozzi's wife became seriously ill and the family was virtually destitute. Pestalozzi became a laughing stock in the town for his failures.

He starts to write

In 1780, Pestalozzi started writing, setting out his theories of education. One of his most famous works, Leonard and Gertrude, was an instant success. It was the first realistic representation of rural life in that part of Europe. It told the story of a woman who exposed corruption and, by her well-ordered home, set a model for the village school and wider community. For 30 years, Pestalozzi lived in virtual isolation on the Neuhof estate, writing about education, politics and economics.

After the French Revolution, Pestalozzi sought and gained government approval to set up a school in Stans for war orphans. He cared for them almost single-handedly and tried to restore their lives. He later said that these exhausting months in 1799 were the happiest of his life. At first there were 50 children but the numbers grew to 80. Pestalozzi commented on the scabies, open sores, ragged clothing, and overall physical plight of these children. Within five months, they were living together happily.

His writing

Pestalozzi's writings include:

- *The Evening House of a Hermit*
- *Leonard and Gertrude* (University Press of the Pacific)
- *How Gertrude Teaches her Children*
- *Swansong and Life's Destiny* (published as a single volume)

His theory

It has been suggested that Pestalozzi 'may fairly be regarded as the starting point of modern educational theory and practice' (1). He believed, like Jean-Jacques Rousseau, that education must be 'according to nature'. For Pestalozzi, however, security in the home was the foundation of happiness and, since it formed the basis of children's reality, was also the foundation for learning.

He believed that all children had an equal right to education and the capacity to profit from it. He attacked conventional education for being dull and too little concerned with interest and experience. He thought that children's innate faculties should be developed in accordance with nature, that they should be encouraged to observe concrete objects. Progress from the familiar to the new should be in a loving and secure environment.

Pestalozzi emphasised the unique nature of the individual and the inner dignity of everyone. He believed that every child has potential but that without love neither physical nor intellectual powers can develop naturally. He wrote that love, work and social interaction were the foundations of development.

Putting the theory into practice

Pestalozzi thought that children should be taught in groups according to their ability, not necessarily their age. The practical elements of his work owe something to Comenius (see pages 4-5) in that he emphasised the importance of the senses and based learning on the familiar. Spelling and reading were practised with moveable letters, pebbles and beans, and even apples and cakes were used for sums and fractions. Only when mathematical ideas were fully understood did Pestalozzi teach children numbers. This was a far cry from the conventional education of the early 1800s.

For Pestalozzi the most important sensory experience was observation. He led what were known as 'object lessons' and linked these to actions since, for him, action must follow perception. He argued that life shapes us and the life that shapes us is not a matter of words but actions – education involves the repetition of actions.

World famous school

But the project took its toll on Pestalozzi's health and the school closed. Another was established in Burgdorf, where he stayed for a number of years but never lost the ambition to set up an industrial school for poor children. These years were invaluable in enabling Pestalozzi to formulate his educational theories which were published in 1801 as How Gertrude Teaches her Children. From 1800 to 1804, Pestalozzi directed the educational establishment at Burgdorf. In 1805 he opened a boarding school at Yverdun. Both schools relied on fee-paying pupils but some poor children were taken in to satisfy Pestalozzi's lifelong wish to educate the poor.

The Yverdun Institute became world famous and drew pupils from all over Europe. It would have up to 250 pupils at any one time. They were given plenty of exercise in the fresh air, nourishing food, had ten lessons a day (starting at six in the morning), enjoyed swimming, tobogganing and long walks. The institute attracted the attention of Friedrich Froebel (see pages 14-16).

But again Pestalozzi's grand plans failed and the institute closed. During its last year he wrote his great political work, To the Innocence, the Earnestness and the Generosity of My Age and My Country.

Towards the end of his life, Pestalozzi wrote constantly about his ideas and theories and in 1825, when he was in his eighties, he returned to Neuhof to concentrate on writing. He died two years later, in 1827.

Johann Pestalozzi

His influence

Friedrich Froebel (see pages 14-16) and Robert Owen (see pages 11-13) both spent time at Yverdun. Froebel in particular was heavily influenced by Pestalozzi's work. Many of the phrases today associated with Froebel (such as 'learning by doing' and 'making the inner outer') were taken from Pestalozzi.

Owen had some criticisms of Yverdun, yet he sent some of his sons to a school which had been set up by one of Pestalozzi's followers because he admired the belief that rich and poor should be educated in similar ways.

The tradition established by Pestalozzi and his wife of taking in underprivileged children has been perpetuated in the Pestalozzi Children's Villages. At the end of the Second World War, the Swiss humanist, Dr Walter Corti (1910-90), wanted to help orphaned and refugee children. He set up a village at Trogen in Switzerland in Pestalozzi's name. In 1957, a second Pestalozzi village was established in East Sussex. Originally, the English school took children from the age of nine whose lives had been devastated by war. Then it helped children from other conflicts, before including Third World countries. Today there is worldwide work in a range of Pestalozzi Children's Villages.

Comment

Pestalozzi was not generally regarded as successful. The schools he established were not open for long. Owen believed that Yverdun was less successful than his school in New Lanark at providing children with life skills. Perhaps Pestalozzi's dream of providing a practical education fell down because he was not entirely practical himself.

Although he built on many of Pestalozzi's theories, Froebel believed that Pestalozzi did not pay enough attention to physical involvement in learning. His occupations and activities were designed to address what he saw as a flaw in Pestalozzi's work.

Reference

(1) Green, J A and Collie, F A *Pestalozzi's Educational Writings* (Edward Arnold 1916) (quote from page 1)

Where to find out more
www.infed.org/thinkers

For more information about the Pestalozzi Children's Villages, visit the website: www.pestalozziworld.com

Robert Owen

PROFILE

Robert Owen, a self-made Welsh businessman, set up the first workplace nursery in Britain at his cotton mills in New Lanark in Scotland. Many of his policies and ideas were ahead of their time.

LINKS

1771	Born in Newtown, Wales
1815	Establishes factory in New Lanark
1816	New Lanark infant school opens, catering for children aged two to six
1818	Visits Pestalozzi at Yverdun
1825	Establishes New Harmony village in USA
1858	Dies

LINKS

- Pestalozzi

His life

In 1815, Robert Owen, a cotton manufacturer, set up a new factory complex in New Lanark in Scotland. Many of his workers were destitute refugees, evicted from the land clearance in the Highlands of Scotland. Owen believed he should provide for their welfare and built housing, social facilities and a school.

He recognised the childcare problems which women workers faced and provided a nursery, known at that time as an infant school. The school was an early attempt to provide group care and education for the very young children of working class parents, and is sometimes described as the first workplace nursery.

His reminders to staff to show 'unceasing kindness, in tone, look, word and action, to all the children without exception' (1) reflect his genuine liking for children. He provided musicians and hired artists to paint murals. He even bought a baby alligator to stimulate interest in natural history and geography. Children stayed at school until the age of ten but classes were also provided for adults.

Owen was a businessman. He claimed that by catering for the needs of families and children his manufacturing profits rose. The workforce was happy and therefore productive. His focus on young children also promised continuing profitability.

He also sought to engineer social change, hoping to replace the competitive and class-bound society of that period with one which was more socialist in outlook. Owen was opposed to child labour and the provision made for children at New Lanark had some influence in changing opinions. The New Lanark nursery attracted many visitors. However, although ideas of combined nursery centres - offering both care and education - were taken up elsewhere in Europe (for example, the ecoles maternelles which began in France in 1848), the idea was not as well received in Britain. Neither employers nor government showed much concern for the welfare of workers.

Robert Owen

In 1818 Owen visited a number of experimental schools in Europe. Amongst them was Pestalozzi's school at Yverdun. Pestalozzi shared with Owen a belief in the importance of early education, of sensory experience and of the environment. Owen is reported to have remarked that Pestalozzi's theory 'was one step beyond the usual routine' (2) but thought that New Lanark was better at ensuring that children had the skills with which to earn a living and at nurturing positive dispositions for learning.

Owen was a social reformer who lived by his own beliefs. He sent some of his sons to a school at Hofwyl in Switzerland which was run by von Fellenberg, a follower of Pestalozzi. He was impressed by the school's philosophy which sought (unusually at the time) to educate rich and poor in a similar way. All children had to tend fields and the aim was to bring different social classes closer together.

In 1825, Robert Owen went to live in America. He had bought a village and created a venture that he called New Harmony. His aim was to establish a 'community of equality' where people lived communally, ate together in the same place and wore similar clothes. Owen never lived there but some of his children did. The constitution included these objectives (3):

- equality of rights, uninfluenced by sex or condition in all adults;
- equality of duties, modified by physical and mental conformation;
- co-operative union, in the business and amusements of life;
- community of property;
- freedom of speech and action;
- sincerity in all our proceedings;
- kindness in all our actions;
- courtesy in all our intercourse;
- order in all our arrangements;
- preservation of health;
- acquisition of knowledge;
- the practice of economy, or of producing and using the best of everything in the most beneficial manner;
- obedience to the laws of the country in which we live.

In both New Lanark and New Harmony radical ideas on the environment, concern for social well-being and a sense of community were seen as being connected to the education not just of young children but of adults as well.

His writing

Robert Owen wrote a vast number of political pamphlets and books. Harrison (4) gives a comprehensive listing of his work. A more recent selection of his work was published in 1993 by Claeys (5).

His theory

Two statements are important in understanding Robert Owen's educational theories (6). They are:

'Man is a compound being, whose character is formed of his constitution or organisation at birth, and of the effects of external

circumstances acting upon that organisation, which effects continue to operate upon and to influence him from birth to death....'

'Nevertheless, the constitution of every infant, except in the case of organic disease, is capable of being formed or nurtured, either into a very inferior or a very superior being, according to the qualities of the external circumstances allowed to influence that constitution from birth.'

Owen believed that the experiences we offer young children have a lifelong impact on the way in which they develop.

Putting the theory into practice

Owen wanted children to be happy and treated with kindness and respect. His expectation was that this kindness would be imitated and that children would be kind to one another.

The schoolroom at New Lanark has been described (7) as being 'furnished with paintings, chiefly of animals, with maps, and often supplied with natural objects from the garden, fields and woods - the examination and explanation of which always excited their curiosity and created an animated conversation between the children and their instructors'.

Children were encouraged to spend many hours each day in the open air and there was a strong emphasis on physical activity and music - singing, marching to music, fife playing and dancing. Dancing lessons began at the age of two and children became highly competent at, what a contemporary writer described as 'all the dances of Europe'. This was said to be because Robert Owen had 'discovered that dancing is one means of reforming vicious habits.... by promoting cheerfulness and contentment... thus diverting attention from things that are vile and degrading' (8).

Books were considered inappropriate for young children. Geography had a 'strong moral undertone, for the children were often reminded that but for an accident of birth they might have been born into a different society with values totally unlike those of their own' (9). The emphasis was on morality, on respecting others and never acting in unkind ways.

His influence

Robert Owen has been described as 'one of the most important and controversial figures of his generation' (10).

The ideas that Owen developed in New Lanark were influential in changing attitudes about child labour. His commitment to education, not just for children but as a lifelong process, was also radical, as were his ideas about the importance of equality.

Comment

Robert Owen's work has been criticised as being rooted in his desire for profit rather than genuine concern for the welfare of his workers and their families. However, his policies were a bold step forward.

References
(1) Whitbread, N *The Evolution of the Nursery-Infant School* (Routledge and Kegan Paul 1972). (Whitbread cites Owen on page 14)
(2) Donnachie, I *Robert Owen: Owen of New Lanark and New Harmony* (Tuckwell Press 2000) (page 149)
(3) Donnachie, I *Robert Owen: Owen of New Lanark and New Harmony* (Tuckwell Press 2000) (page 237)
(4) Harrison, J F C *Robert Owen and the Owenites in Britain and America*
(5) Claeys, G (ed) *Selected Works of Robert Owen* 4 vols
(6) Whitbread, N *The Evolution of the Nursery-Infant School* (Routledge and Kegan Paul 1972) (Whitbread quotes from Owen's book *The New Moral World,* published in 1836, on page 9)
(7) Whitbread, N *The Evolution of the Nursery-Infant School* (Routledge and Kegan Paul 1972) (Morton, 1962, cited by Whitbread on page 10)
(8) Donnachie, I *Robert Owen: Owen of New Lanark and New Harmony* (Tuckwell Press 2000) (Donnachie cites Griscom on page 170)
(9) Donnachie, I *Robert Owen: Owen of New Lanark and New Harmony* (Tuckwell Press 2000) page 169
(10) Donnachie, I *Robert Owen: Owen of New Lanark and New Harmony* (Tuckwell Press 2000) (page ix)

Where to find out more
Robert Owen: Owen of New Lanark and New Harmony
by I Donnachie (Tuckwell Press 2000)

Friedrich Froebel

1782 – 1852

PROFILE

Friedrich Froebel is well known for saying that play is a child's work. He saw childhood as part of nature and steeped in spirituality. His influence is seen today in the emphasis on the play in early childhood education and a child-centred approach to learning.

KEY DATES

1782	Born in Thuringia, Prussia (now Germany)
1808	Teaches at Pestalozzi's school in Switzerland
1813	Serves in the Napoleonic Wars
1816	Sets up own school in Griesheim
1818	Sets up school in Keilhau
1826	*The Education of Man* is published
1852	Dies
1854	Beginning of Froebelian training in England
1857	Froebelian training courses certificated by the Froebel Society for the Promotion of the Kindergarten System

LINKS

- Rousseau
- Pestalozzi
- Chris Athey and schema theory

His life

Friedrich Froebel was born in 1782 in Thuringia, now part of Germany. He was the son of a clergyman and the youngest of five children. His mother died when he was nine months old. When he was ten, he went to live with an uncle who took an interest in him and sent him to school. He enjoyed mathematics and languages but his great passion was nature, particularly plants.

After leaving school he became an apprentice forester. After two years he took some informal courses at Jena University where he developed an appetite for philosophy and a love of intellectual learning. He read widely and studied hard and was influenced by the thinkers of the day. He took a variety of jobs, including land surveyor, estate manager and secretary until his reading led him to an interest in teaching. He spent some time teaching at Pestalozzi's school in Yverdun.

Froebel went to Frankfurt to study architecture but took up teaching after meeting Anton Gruner. Gruner ran what was seen as a progressive school in Frankfurt and he gave Froebel a job there. After further study (interrupted in 1813 by military service during the Napoleonic Wars) at the University of Gottingen, Froebel set up his own school in Griesheim in Thuringia. He was 34.

In 1818, he moved the school to Keilhau in Prussia and began to put his educational theories into practice. Influenced by both Rousseau and Pestalozzi, Froebel believed in child-centred education.

He and the friends with whom he set up the school (together with their families) became an educational community. This is reflected in his writings when he says 'Let us live with our children, let them live with us, so we shall gain through them what all of us need' (1). The school flourished.

At the request of the Swiss government he spent some time training teachers in Switzerland, then began work as head of a new orphanage school there. It was this job that sparked his deep interest in the early years.

Froebel died in 1852. Two years later, The Times and other respected publications published articles about his work and theories.

His writing

Froebel wrote many articles on education, but his writing does not make for easy reading. His most famous work, The Education of Man, was published in 1826. His style was deeply philosophical, reflecting his spiritual and religious beliefs, including his view of the unity of God, man and nature.

Among the best known of his books are:

- *The Education of Man* (Appleton 1887)
- *Mother Play and Nursery Songs*, prose translated by Jarvis, J and songs translated by Dwight, F E (Lee and Shepard 1878)

His theory

Froebel had firm views on play and its place in child development, believing that it fostered enjoyment, emotional well-being and was a fundamental source of benefit.

He insisted that the education of young children was vital to their development as individuals and to social reform. His first kindergarten was called the Child Nurture and Activity Institute. Kindergarten can be translated either as 'children's garden' or 'garden of children'. Both meanings were used by Froebel and reflect his philosophy about young children.

Froebel was the first person to articulate a comprehensive theory on how children learn and give detailed instructions for putting it into practice (2). His work gave rise to the idea of having a philosophy of education (3). His philosophy was founded on the importance of the garden and included notions of mutual respect. This is reflected in his phrase 'at every stage be that stage' - highlighting the idea that children should be allowed to be children, enjoying the things that children enjoy without having to be concerned for what comes next. Froebel also encouraged teachers to 'begin where the learner is'.

He was fascinated by child development and would watch his friends' children play. His observations led him to reflect on the interactions between mothers and babies. He also emphasised the role of the mother in learning and believed that parents should be closely involved in their children's development and education.

Froebel believed that teachers should not teach by rote, as was common at that time, but encourage self-expression through play. As Froebel became more experienced his theory developed and he came to see play as fundamental to children's development and the most spiritual or highest form of activity in which humans (not just children) engage.

He was passionate about the interconnectedness of life, beauty and knowledge. These three forms (as he called them) were connected to aspects of kindergarten provision and included sensory and first-hand experience, nature, music and the arts and mathematics. Spirituality was to be found in everything.

Froebel wanted the kindergarten to be an institution for the 'cultivation of family life, and the forming of national life and even of all humanity' (5).

Putting the theory into practice

Froebel emphasised the fundamental role of women in the education of young children. He deliberately recruited women teachers at a time when teaching was largely seen as male role. This owed much to the deprivation that Froebel believed he had suffered because of his own mother's death. He wrote that the death of his mother influenced his whole future development and described the misery of his early years without a mother.

Play and the outdoor environment were important in a Froebelian kindergarten. Children between the age of one and seven would be encouraged to garden and to enjoy nature and the outdoors. Nature walks were part of the provision he recommended. He believed that space and light were essential to learning.

Teaching at that time was directed and formal but Froebel suggested that children should be encouraged to do something instead of being told or shown. This marked a major step forward. The comparative freedom of outdoor play and gardening were tempered by the rather constrained Gifts and Occupations that Froebel designed (see page 15).

Froebel was among the first educationists to see the value of the sounds produced by different materials or by singing. He saw them as a means of creative expression. He developed songs and rhymes for young children, which he called 'Mother Songs'. These were published in 1878.

His influence

After Froebel died, a number of colleges in England began to offer Froebelian training. In 1857, the Froebel Society for the Promotion of the Kindergarten System began to certificate courses to ensure uniformity of standards. This society was set up by Emily Shirreff and her sister, Maria Grey. Its role was to publicise Froebelian methods and provide teacher training to staff in kindergartens.

Gifts and Occupations

Froebel developed a set of playthings or structured materials which he called Gifts. In The Education of Man, he discussed the use of large sets of blocks (around 500 in all). However, in later writings he does not mention these and instead emphasises the Gifts.

The Gifts consisted of:

Gift 1	A box of six small soft woollen balls or spheres
Gift 2	A wooden cube, cylinder and sphere
Gifts 3	A two-inch cube divided into eight one-inch wooden cubes
Gifts 4-6	Each of these was cut from an eight-inch cube which was divided in different ways, into cubes, half cubes, cuboids, triangles and prisms.

They were presented in a highly structured way. Children had to take the Gift carefully from the box and 'every block within the Gift had to be used and any new construction made by transforming the existing one, rather than knocking it down and starting again' (4). A special table was provided, marked in one-inch squares to encourage careful and symmetrical working. When they had finished, children had to replace the blocks in the box.

Froebel developed graduated exercises which he based on the games he had observed children playing. He promoted the use of soft clay, wet sand, pieces of wood, and drawing with crayons and chalk.

He also designed Occupations to develop children's manual dexterity. These included weaving, paper folding, cutting and sewing on perforated cards.

Friedrich Froebel

The Froebel Educational Institute for training teachers opened in West Kensington in 1894. This later moved to the present site in Roehampton, where the Froebel Institute (together with its Early Childhood Archive Centre) forms part of Roehampton University.

Froebel's work attracted a lot of interest in North America and Europe where large numbers of kindergartens opened, offering provision based on Froebel's teaching.

His work continued to have a strong influence well into the twentieth century, even though Froebelian practice was rarely seen. The progressive ideals of education which grew in the years between the two world wars were firmly rooted in the philosophy which he had developed.

Froebel commented on the first smile as a social action depending not only on the child's development as an individual but on the encouragement of the mother. This is accepted now largely due to our understanding of neuroscience and attachment but it was not a popular view in the nineteenth century.

The aims of the Froebel Society included the desire to educate the public on all matters concerning young children. This continues today. The Froebel Block Play project and Chris Athey's project (see page 50), for example, were funded through the society and have made a major contribution to our understanding of young children.

Comment

Froebel's methods were often misunderstood in this country, perhaps because his work was not translated into English until 1885. The relationship between play and the use of the Gifts and the principles that underpinned them were not always clear. There was a sharp divide between what Froebel said and the intricate instructions that went with the Gifts which made the theory difficult to put into practice.

Froebel recruited women and, it has been suggested, came to overstate the importance of women as teachers of young children.

Froebelian kindergartens were essentially middle class. Despite this, Froebel's methods were adapted for use with disadvantaged children and families as nursery and infant schools were established at the beginning of the twentieth century in inner-city areas. While some writers and theorists of the early twentieth century saw Froebel's theory as having universal application, others felt that it did not address the needs of poor children.

Despite Froebel's emphasis on nature walks, gardening and outdoor play, his work is sometimes criticised for undervaluing the importance of gross motor development. Many of the Gifts and Occupations require high levels of fine motor skill but need to be seen in their historical context.

References
(1) Bruce, T *Early Childhood Education* (Hodder and Stoughton 1987) (Bruce cites Froebel on page 11. The reference is to Froebel's book *The Education of Man*, published in 1887.)
(2) Blackstone, T A *Fair Start: the Provision of Pre-school Education* (Allen Lane 1971)
(3) Aspin, D N 'Friedrich Froebel: visionary, prophet and healer?' *Early Childhood Development and Care* Vol 12 (1983)
(4) Read, J 'A Short History of Children's Building Blocks' in Gura, P (ed) *Exploring Learning* (Paul Chapman Publishing 1992) (Jane Read describes the Gifts on page 5.)
(5) Singer, E *Childcare and the Psychology of Development* (Routledge 1992) (Singer cites Froebel on page 52.)

Where to find out more
Early Childhood Education by T Bruce (Hodder and Stoughton 1987)
'A Short History of Children's Building Blocks' by J Read in *Exploring Learning* edited by P Gura (Paul Chapman Publishing 1992)
Childcare and the Psychology of Development by E Singer (Routledge 1992) (Chapter 4)

Sigmund Freud and psychoanalytic theories

Key figures in psychoanalysis

Psychoanalysis can be defined as a means of helping patients to deal with emotional problems or disorders by probing unconscious thought. Sigmund Freud described it as 'the talking cure'.

Psychoanalytic theories are most commonly associated with Sigmund Freud but a number of other theorists have influenced our understanding of how children learn and develop.

Sigmund Freud emphasised the importance of early experience. Like Piaget, he saw development in stages but the focus of his theory was the role of our unconscious.

Carl Jung developed the idea of introversion and extroversion. He also focused on the unconscious but thought that development was modified by our personal and our collective (or social) unconscious.

Melanie Klein was interested in children. She believed that play gives children a way of expressing fantasies and reliving experiences symbolically. After coming to England, she became close to Susan Isaacs, living and working with her on the Cambridge Evacuation Study during the Second World War. Her work also influenced Winnicott. Klein believed that children used play to symbolise their experiences. Anna Freud disagreed.

Anna Freud, Sigmund Freud's youngest daughter, worked with her father and, following a period of imprisonment by the Gestapo, was allowed to leave Austria and come to Britain in 1938. Sigmund Freud was allowed to leave with his wife and children, including Anna - but his sisters died in a concentration camp. Anna Freud's theories were closely based on those of her father but the focus of her work was child psychology. For her the major differences between working with children and working with adults were that:

- the relationship with the therapist is different since the parents are still of overwhelming importance to the child;
- children are less able to symbolise or talk about their experiences than adults.

PROFILE

Psychoanalytic theories, derived from the work of Sigmund Freud, have generally been more influential in therapy than in education. However, they have some place in education, such as the idea of helping children come to terms with their fears through play.

KEY DATES

1856 - 1939
    Sigmund Freud
    (Moravia, now part of the
    Czech Republic)

1875 - 1961
    Carl Jung (Switzerland)

1882 - 1960
    Melanie Klein (Austria)

1895 - 1982
    Anna Freud, Sigmund Freud's
    youngest daughter (Austria)

1896 - 1971
    Donald Winnicott (England)

1900 – 1980
    Erich Fromm (Germany)

1902 - 1994
    Erik Erikson (Germany)

1913   Founding of London
    (later British)
    Psychoanalytical Society

LINKS

- Isaacs
- Bowlby

Sigmund Freud and psychoanalytic theories

Donald Winnicott was a respected paediatrician and psychoanalyst whose work continues to be influential in Britain and America. His career began in paediatrics but he made many contributions to the development of psychoanalytic theories. Winnicott underlined the importance to children of adult engagement in play (1). His theories focused heavily on mother and child interactions. He wrote about 'good enough mothers' and highlighted the importance of this relationship. He wrote that the mother's face acted as a mirror for the baby since it revealed what she saw or perceived as she looked at her child. He is also known for recognising the way in which transitional objects, such as a piece of a mother's nightdress, act as a symbol of the mother for a child – helping them to bear separation.

Erich Fromm lived in Frankfurt but went to the United States in 1934. His theories were influenced by Sigmund Freud and Karl Marx. He believed that humans have freedom to choose and are not at the mercy of their unconscious motives.

Erik Erikson's ideas are sometimes called psychosocial theory because they cover a life span, with stages running throughout life not ending at adolescence, as do those of Freud and Piaget. Erikson was a pupil and analysand (patient or client) of Anna Freud. He was the first of the psychoanalysts to leave Vienna, following the rise of Nazism. He went to New York, where he had studied, and became well respected and widely known.

Their writings

All of these people were prolific writers. The books below have particular relevance to the development of young children:

- *Psycho-Analytic Treatment of Children, Part 1* Anna Freud (1926)
- *A Symposium on Child Analysis* Melanie Klein (1927)
- *Psycho-Analytic Treatment of Children, Part 2* Anna Freud (1927)
- *Childhood and Society* Erik Erikson (Penguin 1950)
- *The Child, the Family and the Outside World* Donald Winnicott (Penguin 1957)
- *Playing and Reality* Donald Winnicott (Routledge 1971)
- *The Piggle: an account of the psycho-analytic treatment of a little girl* Donald Winnicott (Hogarth 1977)

The eight stages of psychosocial development (Erikson)

Age	Stage	Central crisis
Birth to one year	trust vs mistrust	The first task is to develop a sense of trust or comfort in their caregivers, environment and self. If this crisis is not resolved they may mistrust themselves and others throughout their lives.
1 to 3 years	autonomy vs shame and doubt	During this stage young children are learning to exercise independence. Shame and doubt about one's own ability to act independently may arise if the child is not supported in making choices and decisions.
3 to 6 years	initiative vs guilt	The young child's developing desire to master the environment. Guilt may arise if the child reacts aggressively or irresponsibly.
6 years to adolescence	industry vs inferiority	Children are keen to master intellectual and social challenges but failures may lead to feelings of inferiority and incompetence.
Adolescence (12 to 20 years)	identity vs identity diffusion	Adolescents who fail to explore their own identity because of the demands of parents or others may remain confused.
Young adulthood (20 to 40 years)	intimacy vs isolation	The task at this stage is to establish an intimate relationship with another. Difficulties in resolving earlier crises will affect the individual's success in achieving intimacy.
Middle adulthood (40 to 60 years)	generativity vs stagnation	The central task is to create something - such as children or art. Failure to achieve can lead to the feeling that life has no meaning.
Old age (60 years onwards)	Integrity vs despair	The task is to look back and assess our lives. The person who has been successful in earlier stages can derive a sense of integrity.

Their theories

According to Freud, development occurs as we struggle to balance the demands of the id (the instinctive, pleasure-seeking part of our personality) with those of the superego (the structure within our personality which carries our conscience, derived from the values of our parents and the wider society within which we live). The third part of the personality, the ego, attempts to maintain the balance by, for example, preventing us from acting anti-socially and helping us to find socially acceptable ways to satisfy the id.

Like Piaget, Freud proposed a staged theory of development. The five stages in what is termed psychosexual development were the oral, anal, phallic, latent and genital stages.

Anna Freud and Melanie Klein were interested in psychoanalysis in relation to children. They disagreed over the extent to which play could be successfully used in analysing young children whose normal emotional development had been blocked. Anna Freud was critical of Klein's view that children's free play could be interpreted in a similar way to that used for free association with adults. They also differed in their understanding of children's superego.

Winnicott was influenced by Klein and praised her teaching saying '[I was] astounded by the insight which psychoanalysis gave into the lives of children... I had no idea that what was being taught me was highly original. The thing was that it made sense, and joined up my case history detail with psychoanalytical theory.... For her a specific play with the toys was a projection from the child's psychic reality which is localised by the child, localised inside the self and the body [and which] provides glimpses into the child's inner world' (2).

The most well-known aspect of Winnicott's theory is the transitional object, such as a favourite blanket or well-loved teddy. Winnicott (3) described transitional objects as 'the first thing in the world that belongs to the infant, and yet is not part of the infant'.

Erikson, whose influences mainly came from Anna Freud, proposed three systems which make up the development of the individual:

the somatic system, responsible for all aspects of human biology necessary for healthy functioning;

the ego system, which includes the processes necessary for thinking and reasoning;

the societal system, the processes by which an individual becomes part of their society, culture or community.

For Erikson, psychosocial development has eight stages through which all humans pass, each of which has a central dilemma or crisis. The chart on page 18 (4) sets out the stages and accompanying crises.

Putting the theories into practice

Many of the psychoanalytic theorists did not work in school settings. However, the central tenet of many psychoanalytic theories is that children must be supported in working through their emotional or psychological crises in order to develop a sense of emotional well-being and mental health. The influence of this fundamental aspect of their work can be seen in practice in the early years through the provision made for role play which, in part, helps children to play out fears and anxieties.

Many group settings acknowledge young children's emotional needs through general free play and providing art materials to encourage creative expression (5).

Other aspects of common practice in the early years which can be traced to psychoanalytic theories include (6):

- Transitional objects enable children to maintain a link with comfortable and familiar people and contexts. Practitioners acknowledge the importance of transitional objects when they encourage children to bring their favourite toys and comforters from home as a link between family and setting.

- A key person approach supports the development of security and intimacy, vital to the healthy development of young children.

- Staff discussions can help to raise awareness of processes such as transference, projection of feelings and the need for containment and emotional holding. (For more information about these terms, read Key Times for Play by Manning-Morton and Thorp.)

A number of actions, based on the first three stages of Erikson's theory, can support children's healthy development (7). Practitioners are paying attention to Erikson's stage of trust/ distrust when they:

- hold babies close and share warm physical contact with them when they are being fed;
- respond quickly when babies are distressed.

Awareness of autonomy/shame or doubt are reflected when practitioners:

- give children simple but genuine choices;
- set clear, consistent and reasonable boundaries;
- accept and understand children's swings between independence and dependence.

Erikson's third stage of initiative/guilt is reflected when practitioners:

- encourage children to be independent;
- focus on what children can do, not on the mistakes they make;

- set realistic expectations;
- make the curriculum relevant and based on action.

The influence of psychoanalytic theories

Freud's theory drew attention to the importance of early experience and the unconscious in relation to the development of personality. His work has inspired many others and led to a new way of viewing human development. However, in the context of education, it is the work of Erikson, Freud's student in Vienna, that has been particularly influential.

Erikson created a wider and more educationally relevant theory of psychodynamics by integrating social and cultural factors into his writing. His work also stimulated interest in self-identity and adolescence.

Comment

Freud viewed the development of girls and women from a male perspective, labelling the second stage of development as 'phallic' and thinking of girls' motivation only in terms of 'penis envy'. His theories are based on methods such as dream analysis and free association which are not open to scientific verification.

Erikson's theory could be said to lack coherence and his idiosyncratic use of terms like generativity make his work difficult to understand. The theory is not open to scientific investigation nor does it make clear how development occurs.

References

(1) Manning-Morton, J and Thorp, M (2003) *Key Times for Play* (Open University Press)

(2) Smith, L (1985) *To Understand and to Help: the life and work of Susan Isaacs* (1885-1948) This quote is taken from page 196.

(3) Manning-Morton, J and Thorp, M (2003) *Key Times for Play* (Open University Press) (This quote is taken from page 167 of Winnicott's book entitled *The Child, the Family and the Outside World* which was published in 1957. It is cited by Manning-Morton and Thorp on page 26.)

(4) Keenan, T (2002) *An Introduction to Child Development* (Sage Publications) (adapted from pages 22-23)

(5) MacNaughton, G (2003) *Shaping Early Childhood* (Open University Press)

(6) Manning-Morton, J and Thorp, M (2003) *Key Times for Play* (Open University Press)

(7) Mooney, C G (2000) *Theories of Childhood: an introduction to Dewey, Montessori, Erikson, Piaget and Vygotsky* (Redleaf Press)

Where to find out more
The Erik Erikson Reader R Coles (ed) (W W Norton and Co 2000)
Key Times for Play J Manning-Morton and M Thorp (Open University Press 2003) (see Chapter 2)

Websites:
www.mythsandlogos.com/Winnicott.html
www.psychematters.com/bibliographies

His life

John Dewey was born in 1859 in Vermont into a family of farmers. After gaining a PhD at John Hopkins University he became a professor of philosophy at the University of Michigan. In 1886 he married one of his students, Alice Chipman, and they worked together to explore ways of improving education. Eight years later they moved to Chicago where Dewey took a job teaching philosophy, psychology and educational theory. He established a laboratory school there which attracted worldwide attention.

Questions that Dewey struggled to answer in his observations, lectures and writings included (1):

- How do we best introduce children to subject matter?
- Should we have mixed age classes?
- How can we best plan?
- How can support staff and teachers work best together?
- How should children be taught to think?

His writing

John Dewey's best known publications include:

- My Pedagogic Creed (1897) which set out many of his ideas (2).
- School for Tomorrow, with Evelyn Dewey (Dutton 1915)
- Democracy and Education (Free Press 1916)
- How We Think: a Reinstatement of the Relation of Reflective Thinking to the Educative Process (Henry Regnery 1933)

His theory

Dewey's theory was that:

- children learn by doing (a sentiment developed by Froebel);
- education should be based on real-life situations;

Aspect of theory	Dewey's words from My Pedagogic Creed
Importance of social interaction	True education comes through the stimulation of the child's powers by the demands of the social situations in which he finds himself.
Need to develop the curriculum from children's interests	The child's own instinct and powers furnish the material and give the starting point for all education.
As long as people are alive they are learning	I believe that education... is a process of living and not preparation for future living.
The value and culture of family and community should be reflected in the life of the school.	The school life should grow gradually out of the home life.... it is the business of the school to deepen and extend the child's sense of values bound up in his home.
Teachers are not just teaching children as individuals - they are helping children to live in society and shaping society as a whole	I believe that the teacher is engaged, not simply in the training of individuals, but in the formation of a proper social life.

John Dewey

experimentation and independent thinking should be fostered. He saw children as being characterised by curiosity, similar to scientists.

Putting the theory into practice

At the heart of Dewey's view of education are teachers who:

- have good general knowledge;
- know their children well;
- want to continue learning;
- observe children and plan from what they learn of them.

For Dewey having fun is not enough. He wanted children to have opportunities to:

- develop their own interests;
- work in ways that match their age and stage of development;
- engage in activities and experiences which contribute to their understanding and appreciation of their world.

Dewey is most closely associated with a project approach, developing cross-curricular ways of learning. Mooney (3) gives an example of what she claims Dewey would regard as 'an educational experience'. She describes a kindergarten where the teacher had invited a parent to come and make ice cream with the children. The recipe had been in the family for generations. The mother took the children to a nearby lake and the old ice house which had been used before the days of refrigeration and helped them to make ice cream as it had been made 'in the olden days'. Children discussed their favourite ice creams and visited a factory - they took photographs, drew pictures, collected recipes and followed up a host of interests. The teacher's role is described as follows (4):

'The teacher observed and asked questions to find out what the children already knew. She set up experiences for them to discover things they didn't already know. She used her knowledge of development to plan (a) curriculum that was age appropriate and she documented the children's learning to support her understanding of their thinking. The success of the project is measured by the fact that it led into the next area of study. The children were left curious, wanting more, and confident in their ability to dive in and satisfy their curiosity.'

His influence

The many progressive educational movements which sprang up in England in the first half of the twentieth century acknowledged their debt to Dewey. Susan Isaacs, for example, admired his work. His work influenced a government report (the Hadow Report on Nursery and Infant Schools) published in 1933 and more than 30 years later, in 1967, there were echoes of his influence in the Plowden Report. In 1897, Dewey wrote 'I believe that education... is a process of living and not preparation for future living'. The Plowden Report states, in remarkably similar language, that 'a school is not merely a teaching shop... it is a community in which children learn to live first and foremost as children and not as future adults'.

Dewey has been credited with developing the notion of reflective professional practice (5). He made a distinction between 'routinised' and 'reflective' teaching and he identified stages in reflection which include:

- perplexity, confusion, doubt;
- a tentative interpretation;
- a careful survey;
- a consequent elaboration; and
- testing the hypothesis.

On a more practical level, Dewey is said to have been responsible for project approaches linking learning across the curriculum.

Comment

Project approaches have been criticised as leading to trivialisation. This might occur if the other aspects of Dewey's philosophy are not given enough weight. The reflective practitioner would guard against trivialisation by evaluating learning.

References
(1) Mooney, C G (2000) *Theories of Childhood: an Introduction to Dewey, Montessori, Erikson, Piaget and Vygotsky* (Redleaf Press) (These points are based on Mooney, citing Tanner.)
(2) Mooney sets out these ideas on page 4 of her book.
(3) Also described in *Mooney* (2000).
(4) This is from *Mooney* (2000), page 18.
(5) Pollard, A (2002) *Readings for Reflective Teaching* (Continuum) (Pollard cites Dewey on pages 4-5)

Where to find out more
Theories of Childhood: an Introduction to Dewey, Montessori, Erikson, Piaget and Vygotsky C G Mooney (Redleaf Press 2000)

Website:
www.infed.org/thinkers/et-dewey.htm

Margaret McMillan

Her life

Margaret McMillan and her older sister, Rachel, were born in Westchester County, New York after her parents had emigrated there from Scotland. There was a younger sister but she died of scarlet fever in 1865, aged three, just a few days before their father. Margaret survived the illness but it left her deaf. She didn't recover her hearing until she was 14.

The mother took the remaining sisters back to Scotland, where they lived with her parents in Inverness. McMillan later wrote that it was as though their mother was ashamed of widowhood and that she 'passed into shadow'.

In 1878, aged 18, McMillan was sent to Frankfurt to study music. She returned to Edinburgh a year later to be a governess. In 1881, she went to Switzerland and studied in Geneva and Lausanne as a trainee teacher. She came back in 1883 and worked in England as a governess.

Political writing

She started to take an interest in politics, writing a series of articles for the Christian Socialist magazine. The first was prompted by the London dock strike of 1889. She wrote about things that preoccupied her for the rest of her life - the plight of the poor and their ability to change their lives. McMillan joined the Fabian Society, a left-wing think tank, and was soon speaking all over the country. She soon gained a reputation as an orator and propagandist.

In 1893, McMillan found a job teaching adult education in Bradford and became a member of the Independent Labour Party. In 1894, she was elected onto the Bradford School Board.

Her arrival in Bradford coincided with a period of high unemployment. McMillan was appalled on her visits to schools by the poverty that children lived in. She described the children as dirty, ill-fed and wretched. She began to advise parents on hygiene and nutrition and became a local expert in the health, education and well-being of young children.

McMillan took on more lecture tours - she was a charismatic speaker - and continued with her political writing.

Health and hygiene

In the 1900s, McMillan's work focused on the national medical inspection of children. In 1901, she resigned from the Bradford School Board, following a period of illness, and moved to London, where her sister Rachel was working in a home for young girls. Their interest in the physical health of working class families was widely shared. A high proportion of the recruits to fight in the Boer War were deemed unfit and this alerted many to the poor health of poor families and alarmed them.

In 1903, McMillan became manager of a group of Deptford schools and wrote articles to educate the public about child development, physiology and hygiene. Her public lectures continued and in 1904 she became a member of the Froebel Society which had been set up to train teachers in Froebelian methods (see page 50).

She opened a small experimental clinic at Bow, funded by a wealthy American philanthropist. This later moved to Deptford where it served a group of schools. The Deptford Centre included a clinic. Small operations, such as the removal of adenoids, could be carried out there and a remedial gym improved children's health and strength. From 1911 the provision included a night camp which aimed to improve the health of children in danger of contracting tuberculosis. For nine months of the year, girls between the ages of six and 14 were able to sleep outdoors in a churchyard.

PROFILE

Some argue that Margaret McMillan invented the nursery school. At the beginning of the twentieth century, she set up an open-air camp to nurture underprivileged children with her sister, Rachel. From this she developed the idea of the nursery school with open access to a garden.

KEY DATES

1860	Born in New York, USA
1865	Moves to Scotland with her mother and sister Rachel, following the death of her father and younger sister
1881	Studies in Switzerland
1883	Goes to England to work as governess
1894	Elected to the Bradford School Board
1903	Becomes manager of the Deptford Centre
1917	Sister Rachel dies
1923	Elected President of the Nursery Schools Association
1930	Rachel McMillan Training College opens
1931	Dies in Harrow

LINKS

- Froebel
- Owen

Margaret McMillan

By 1914, the number of places available had trebled, boys were included and the beginnings of an open-air baby camp, catering for 29 young children, had been set up. By 1917, the Rachel McMillan Nursery School had been established, with places for 100 children. There was a strong emphasis on being outdoors. The classrooms were - and still are (the school is part of the London Borough of Greenwich's early years provision) called shelters; there was a large and attractive garden and even when the weather was bad, the classroom verandahs gave children the chance to benefit from fresh air and space. A medical supervisor reported on the marked improvement in children's physical and mental well-being.

Expert in nursery education

By the end of the First World War, Margaret McMillan was considered an expert in nursery education and in 1923 she was elected president of the Nursery Schools Association.

McMillan never married nor had children. When her sister died in 1917 she attempted to adopt two small boys that had been left in their care in 1915. Their father, a Lancashire miner, had left them at the Deptford Centre on his way to the front. The boys had been taken into their home and, when Rachel died, Margaret travelled widely in occupied France in an attempt to find the father and gain his permission for adoption. He refused.

Care and education

In her book, The Nursery School, McMillan wrote that hundreds of thousands of children were in dire need of education and nurture in the early years. She provided a mixture of care and education - the school was open from 8.00am until 5.30pm. She believed children performed badly at school because they were poorly prepared for learning in the early years. She stressed that in the open-air nursery children had no examinations to sit, no formal structure to the day but had time to play, to run free in open spaces, feel the sun and the wind and explore the natural world.

In 1930, the year before she died, Margaret McMillan set up a training college, adjacent to the Rachel McMillan Nursery School. Teacher training continued at the college for around 50 years.

Her writing

Margaret McMillan began writing towards the end of the nineteenth century. Her writings – books and articles - focused on young children and had a Christian and a socialist slant. In 1904 she wrote Education through the Imagination and followed this with The Economic Aspects of Child Labour and Education in 1905. Her most influential book in this country has been The Nursery School (first published in 1919 and revised in 1930).

Her theory

The theories which led Margaret McMillan and her sister, Rachel, to work with young children were rooted in action. Their political and religious beliefs led them to look for ways of alleviating the effects of poverty. This is reflected in the range of work they did to improve the health and well-being of children.

Their educational philosophy drew on Froebel's work and placed a great emphasis on the importance of the garden. The sisters wrote of the importance of time and space in young children's development.

Their focus on health and on children being able to express themselves was so that they could take their place in society. Baths, wholesome meals, fresh air and exercise were all intended to improve children's well-being.

Putting the theory into practice

The nursery school that Margaret McMillan developed in Deptford has large and beautiful gardens. The 'shelters' or classrooms were built with verandahs and with windows that folded back so that the rooms were light and airy. They all had a bath. McMillan wrote that 'Children want space at all ages. But from the age of one to seven, space, that is ample space, is almost as much wanted as food and air. To move, to run, to find things out by new movement, to feel one's life in every limb, that is the life of early childhood'. (1)

The free play associated with Froebel was encouraged here but McMillan felt that neither Froebel nor Pestalozzi had faced up to the problems that affected the lives of the poor. She wrote that (2) children needed experience 'just as they need food... gay and varied music and dancing, with tales and play but above all free movement and experience'.

A routine of regular meals and sleep times was established as well as times for children to run and play.

Her influence

Margaret and Rachel McMillan had many political allies and were highly influential. Their high profile brought the needs of young children to the attention of many who might not otherwise have been interested in or concerned about nurseries.

The establishment of the school medical service and the school meals service, which were brought about through the work of the McMillans, had a long-lasting impact in the UK.

Their emphasis on the nursery school as an open-air institution influenced how nursery schools were built throughout the first half of the twentieth century. The overall approach adopted by Margaret McMillan was seen as exemplary. The work of the school in Deptford was praised in a government report on nursery education published in 1933 (the Hadow Report on Nursery and Infant Schools).

Comment

The McMillan sisters believed that greater economies could be achieved through large-scale institutions and that there was likely to be more widespread provision if it was not too expensive. Others thought it was inappropriate for young children to be in large institutions.

Criticisms were also made of the long hours offered at the school, which was open from 8.00 in the morning until 5.30 each day. This, with the apparently middle class values displayed in the school, such as putting flowers on the table, was seen by some as professionalising parenting. When McMillan was elected president of the Nursery Schools Association in 1923, she suggested that all children from two to seven years of age who are in day care settings should be looked after by fully qualified specialist teachers. She wrote that:

'Underlying all mental and bodily development lies the need for free activity. Without it neither healthy growth of body and spirit, nor training in self-control is possible.... Free activity involves the provision of spontaneous and purposeful activity in spacious open-air conditions ... as well as an atmosphere of love, joy and freedom... the daily routine must provide for the right alternation of rest and activity through the day... it is undesirable to accept the hours of the ordinary school day as the limit for nursery school.'

References
(1) From Margaret McMillan's book *The Nursery School* (see below) and cited by Curtis in *The History of Education in Great Britain*, published by the University Tutorial Press (5th edition) in 1963.
(2) From Margaret McMillan's book *The Nursery School* (first published in 1919 by Dent and revised in 1930).

Where to find out more
Margaret McMillan, *The Children's Champion* G Lowndes (Museum Press 1960)

Rudolf Steiner

1861 – 1925

KEY DATES

1861	Born in Austria
1919	First Steiner-Waldorf school established
1925	Dies First Steiner-Waldorf school opens in England

His life

Rudolf Steiner was born in the village of Kraljevec, Austria (now Croatia). At university he concentrated on maths, physics and chemistry but wrote his final thesis on philosophy.

He worked first in Weimar and then Berlin, where he was involved in publishing. He gave courses on history and natural science and offered practical training in public speaking. However, he was not involved in any of the political groups which flourished in Berlin in the late nineteenth century, under the influence of Karl Marx.

Steiner was interested in spirituality and established a 'science of the spirit', that he called anthroposophy. Albert Schweitzer, an early twentieth century philosopher, was impressed by Steiner's philosophical writings and views. A World Anthroposophical Society still exists with its headquarters in Switzerland and followers in the United States of America. It is concerned with the human struggle for inner freedom.

The workers at the Waldorf-Astoria cigarette factory in Stuttgart asked Steiner to form a school for their children and in 1919 the first Steiner-Waldorf school was founded. Today there are 1,087 nurseries and 640 schools in 50 countries for children aged three to eighteen.

His writing

The Steiner Waldorf Fellowship, Rudolf Steiner Publishing Company and the Anthroposophic Press have published some of Steiner's writings. These include:

- The Renewal of Education through the Science of the Spirit, published in 1981 by Kolisho Archive publications for the Steiner Waldorf Schools Fellowship (from lectures given in 1920)

- Man and the World of the Stars published by Anthroposophic Press (from lectures given in 1922)
- The Education of the Child in the Light of Anthroposophy, republished in 1995 by the Rudolf Steiner Publishing Company
- The Education of the Child, published by Anthroposophic Press (originally published in 1907)

His theory

Rudolf Steiner wanted to create an education which gave children clarity of thought, sensitivity of feeling and strength of will.

Steiner's theory centred on all aspects of growth and development including spirituality. He aimed for all children to experience both arts and sciences and a balanced experience of what he described as 'thinking, feeling and willing'.

Steiner's philosophy sprang from the idea that there are three seven-year cycles of development. Education needs to work with the unfolding abilities and changing needs of the child at each stage. These stages, he claimed, connect with the development of the all-round human qualities of thinking, feeling and willing:

- From birth to seven the active or will predominates;
- From seven to 14 the affective or feeling predominates;
- From 14 to 21, the cognitive or thinking ability predominates.

Steiner believed that children who have suffered from pressure to succeed intellectually at too early an age often lack the motivation to learn for themselves. The avoidance of formal learning springs from a desire to protect the faculties of feeling and willing.

Putting the theory into practice

The environment in Steiner-Waldorf schools is carefully structured to foster personal and social development. During the early years, teaching is by example and learning is cross-curricular without subject boundaries. The pace of learning is set by the child.

Play and imitation are important. Play strengthens the imagination and supports all aspects of development. It also enables children to concentrate, be inventive and adaptable. Steiner teachers believe that these faculties are at their peak from birth to seven and are the main way of learning. They are fostered and respected.

The curriculum combines creativity and practical activity. There is an emphasis on meaningful life experiences such as gardening, cooking, cleaning and an expectation that children will learn from adults as they bake bread, carve spoons and generally go about their daily work.

Up to the age of seven, teachers avoid showing children printed words. Formal schooling does not begin until this age. Mathematics might take place through cooking. Thinly sliced carrots make natural circles. Carrots can be cut, chopped, cubed and counted before being eaten in soup. All mathematical activities arise naturally in response to the demands of the day: flour is weighed, plates and bowls are counted, food is shared. Mathematics is encountered, not in abstract but in practical, human terms.

There is a focus on the spoken word. Stories are told rather than read, creating an appreciation of the human voice and the beauty and rhythm of language, extending vocabulary and supporting the development of memory and imagination. Steiner teachers believe that stories, songs, poems, puppets and movement provide the best possible introduction to literacy.

During each day some time is dedicated to free creative play. Songs, stories, poems and puppet shows together with eurhythmy – a system of movement with language and music that is characteristic of Steiner approaches - are seen as contributing to children's development.

Steiner-Waldorf kindergartens identify rhythm as an important education principle. They argue that children need the reassurance of continuity and that regular events should punctuate the year, week and day. Seasonal activities celebrate the cycles of the year. Each week has its own regular rhythm of recurring activities - baking day, painting day, gardening day. Every day has its own smaller rhythms. These are believed to help the child feel secure and know what to expect; a tidy-up song for example might signal the end of one activity and the start of another. Each day has a special time - a quiet moment to experience reverence.

There is a rhythmic shift between the child's time (creative play, outside time) and the teacher's time (circle time, story), which in the early years is kept short. Steiner believed that working with rhythm helps children to live with change, to find their place in the world and to begin to understand the past, present and future. Repetition also establishes continuity and aids the development of memory which is strengthened by recurring experiences. Daily, weekly and yearly events are remembered and anticipated a second time around. Stories are told not just once but many times.

The kindergarten is designed to be a warm and friendly place with a homelike environment. Parental involvement is high.

The physical environment is important. 'The teacher attempts to engage the child's whole being in what they do, in as an artistic way as possible, by providing a warm and joyful environment in which the child can feel nurtured and at ease, happy to explore and play, be busy and be still...... The room is painted and in a warm colour, has few hard rectangular corners, and is often furnished with soft muslins to mark off a different area, or draped over a window to give a softer quality of light. The quality of sound is that of human voices rather than of mechanical toys. The materials in the room are natural and are at children's level, and stored in aesthetic containers such as simple baskets or wooden boxes which may themselves be incorporated into the play (1).'

His influence

The philosophy which underpins the work of Steiner-Waldorf schools is widely respected. Its emphasis on imaginative play and not introducing children to print until they are seven flies in the face of mainstream practice which favours an early introduction to books. It provides food for thought for reflective practitioners, encouraging them to pause and reconsider why they do what they do (2).

Comment

Children have enormous understanding of print at a very early stage – they see words in their environment not just in books. To ignore this in the early years could be seen as not recognising and building on children's previous experience.

The absence of clear academic aims is at odds with current mainstream practice. It may be seen as indulgent and insufficiently challenging and yet accounts of practice identify high levels of engagement in play and imaginative activity as well as everyday activities such as cooking.

References

(1) Drummond, M J, Lally, M and Pugh, G (eds) (1989) *Working with children: developing a curriculum for the early years* (National Children's Bureau) (The quote comes from page 59.)
(2) Howard Gardner in his book *The Unschooled Mind* (Fontana Press 1991) states that it is no accident that in most societies children do not begin statutory schooling until the age of six or seven, since it is only at that stage that they can usefully deal with symbol systems such as print.

Where to find out more

'Another way of seeing: perceptions of play in a Steiner Kindergarten' by Drummond, M J in *Early Education Transformed* Abbot, L and Moylett, H (eds) (Falmer Press, 1999)
Rudolf Steiner Education Edmunds, L F (Rudolf Steiner Press 1986)
Working with Children: Developing a Curriculum for the Early Years Drummond, M J, Lally, M and Pugh, G (NES in association with the National Children's Bureau 1989)

Websites:
www.steinercollege.org.uk
www.steinerbooks.org/aboutrudolf.html

Maria Montessori

Her life

Montessori's father was a soldier and later a civil servant. Her mother was from a wealthy family and well educated.

Montessori was a diligent student, good at mathematics. She enrolled at the University of Rome to become a doctor - unheard of for a woman in Italy at that time. On graduating, she took up a post as an assistant at San Giovanni Hospital and became interested in the welfare of deprived children and in particular what were then called 'idiot children'. She began to study the subject and the writings of Edouard Seguin about mentally defective children.

Special schools

This in turn nurtured an interest in education. She read all the major works on educational theory of the previous 200 years and became convinced of the need for special schools for mentally retarded and emotionally disturbed children.

By 1900, Maria Montessori was well known and respected for her

- teaching as a physician,
- teaching in a school of education,
- achievement of an award for outstanding services to hospitals and
- directorship of a school in Rome, teaching and training in the care and education of mentally deficient children.

But in that year she gave birth to a son, which led to her withdrawal from many aspects of public life. The father was a colleague, but this was kept secret or her career would have been finished. She maintained some contact with her son and gave up her directorship of the school and many of her medical connections. She returned to the University of Rome to study anthropology, experimental psychology, educational psychology and educational philosophy.

She would visit elementary schools to see how children were being taught and came to believe that the methods of education which she had developed in her work with children with mental disability were appropriate for all children. She thought that they would offer children better opportunities for personal growth and development.

In 1904, Montessori was appointed to set up a university course for students in the Faculty of Natural Sciences and Medicine in the Pedagogic School of the University of Rome. She stayed there until 1908 but also taught at the Instituto Superiore di Magistero Femminile until 1906. At that time she was appointed to the Board of Examiners for the degree of natural science in anthropology, a considerable academic distinction. All the while she continued to practise in hospitals and clinics and to publish a range of professional papers..

Casa dei Bambini

Her next project was to set up the first Casa dei Bambini or children's house in a slum district of Rome as part of an urban regeneration project. The children there were given simple things to play with and the staff were told only to observe children at play and not to intervene. She was astonished at the results - children who had been sullen and withdrawn started to show interest in the objects they had been given to play with. There were wooden cylinders which fitted into a stand, cubes to build into a tower and different shapes to fit into holes on a wooden tray. Staff noticed that children became absorbed in these objects and preferred to play with them rather than the dolls and balls or little wagons. Montessori described the children as changing from timid and wild to social, communicative and joyous.

PROFILE

Maria Montessori was the first woman in Italy to receive a medical degree. She is famous for developing an approach to early childhood education that still carries her name.

KEY DATES

1870	Born in Ancona, Italy
1886-1890	Studies modern foreign languages, natural science and mathematics
1894	Specialises in paediatrics
1896	Graduates as the first female doctor in Italy
1900	Son born
1904	Appointed to Faculty of Natural Sciences and Medicine in the Pedagogic School of the University of Rome
1907	Opens first Casa Dei Bambini (children's house) in Rome
1913	100 Montessori schools in USA
1922	Becomes government inspector of schools in Rome
1934	Leaves Italy to escape from Mussolini's Fascist regime
1952	Dies in the Netherlands

LINKS

- Isaacs

Maria Montessori

What is now known as the Montessori method began as responses to the observations made of children in the Casa dei Bambini. Over time Montessori opened more Casa dei Bambini and extended her methods to older children and to children from more affluent families.

Her book, The Montessori Method, describes every aspect of a child's life at Montessori school, from what the child should eat for lunch to how the teachers should dress and how the room should be set out. The book was widely read and translations were published in various countries. More schools opened, a Montessori Society was founded in Rome, and in 1911, Montessori visited America. Educators travelled from all over the world to visit the Casa dei Bambini and spread the word on their return.

Bertram Hawker, a wealthy Englishman, visited Montessori. He was so impressed by what he saw that he established the first English Montessori class in his home in East Runton, Norfolk.

The Montessori movement

At the age of 40, Maria gave up all other work to devote her life to the schools and societies of the Montessori movement. The movement had become a business in which Maria was involved in copyright of materials, official certification and giving lectures and writing.

Her first visit to London was in 1919. Huge crowds greeted her arrival at Charing Cross station. Newspapers described her arrival as the beginning of a great era for children in this country. The planned training course for 250 people brought more than 2,000 applications for places.

Montessori was so popular in Holland that the system became firmly established in both public and private schools there. Amsterdam became the headquarters of the Montessori movement and it was in Holland where she made her final home with her son, Mario. Although they were reunited when he was 15 years of age, she did not acknowledge him as her son until her death.

She died in Holland of a brain haemorrhage, just a few months before her 82nd birthday.

Her writing

Montessori's method was described in detail in her book The Montessori Method (published in 1912 by Heinemann).

Other publications include:

- The Absorbent Mind (ABC Clio Ltd 1988) (First published in 1949)

Her theory

Montessori claimed that her philosophy was based on scientific observations. She observed that education begins from birth and that children experience periods of special sensitivity during which they are eager to learn. The Montessori classroom accommodates children of mixed ages and is designed to meet children's needs at periods when they are most interested and motivated. The approach aims to harness children's natural ability to learn and offers concrete experiences and materials to explain abstract principles.

Montessori wrote that 'the child can only be free when the adult becomes an acute observer. Any action of the adult that is not a response to the children's observed behaviour limits the child's freedom' (1).

Her observations suggested to her that children:

- Learn through movement, particularly the movement of the hand which she believed was linked to the development of intelligence.
- Enjoy learning in an environment designed to meet their needs.
- Learn best through the senses. For example, she developed methods of teaching children letters and numbers by cutting out shapes in sandpaper. She wrote that the senses should come first, then the intellect.
- Can learn to read, write and count at an early age - although she believed that these should only be introduced when children showed interest.
- Respond to educational opportunities in an environment which is prepared to meet their special sensitivities for learning. She said that children have 'sensitive periods' when their senses are ready to learn new ideas and teachers should be ready to spot these times in a child's development.
- Reveal a spontaneous self-discipline within a prepared environment.

Putting the theory into practice

The curriculum in today's Montessori nurseries is based on Montessori's principles of education. It aims to support all aspects of the child's personal and social development. The main curriculum areas are:

Daily living skills which aim to provide foundations for learning centred around:

- care for the environment;
- care for oneself as an individual;
- care for others in the community.

Education of the senses which aim to develop skills for learning. By observing, understanding and exploring the world through the senses, the child learns how to classify, discriminate, evaluate and sequence.

Language development which aims to develop the four aspects of language - spoken language, listening, writing and reading. Self-expression and communication are vital elements of all four. A characteristic of Montessori teaching is the phonetic method which is used to teach the sounds of the letters of the alphabet followed by word building exercises which lead to phonetic reading, then total reading.

Number concepts which aim to provide a concrete understanding of the concepts of number and mathematics in the environment. The child progresses through an understanding of number to the structure and processes of the decimal system.

Science and exploration of the wider world which aims to provide experiences of the natural world including the plant and animal kingdoms, people, events and cultures. This section of the curriculum integrates mathematical, linguistic, sensory and daily living activities. Children are given the opportunity to experience and create in areas relating to cultures - art, music, craft, drama, dance and physical education. These aspects are said to enable children to develop their imaginative responses and their creative self-expression.

Those who work in Montessori schools claim that the method leads to children who are developed in a balanced way, who are decision-makers, who are confident and independent.

Maria Montessori introduced small-scale furniture for children. She had child-sized lightweight furniture, including little armchairs and washstands, specially made. Gardening, gymnastics, caring for plants and pets were added to the daily activities. The children were free to move about and to choose what interested them, within certain boundaries set down by the staff. Materials were placed so that children could get out and use the equipment they needed. They were given relatively long uninterrupted periods of time in which to follow their interests or to carry out their tasks.

Her influence

Montessori was feted when she came to London in 1919 - a large reception was held at the Savoy. She was invited to lecture widely and the courses she offered were oversubscribed. Her success with supporting the education of what were then known as 'subnormal' children led her to apply her methods and equipment to the development of all young children.

Her influence continued in London in state schools up to the Second World War. Montessori equipment and the small-scale furniture she introduced were to be found in infant schools throughout the city.

The Montessori method continues to be favoured around the world. It is clearly structured and offers clear guidance to practitioners.

Comment

The prescriptive nature of the Montessori method is often criticised. It cannot be easily adapted or updated.

One of the greatest difficulties with the method is its rejection of the role of play and imagination in learning. Montessori was dealing with severely disadvantaged children. She believed that they needed to learn through meaningful tasks and that imaginative play would distract them from the real world. She did not see play as an important part of learning.

Susan Isaacs was critical of the phonic approach to reading that Montessori advocated. She quoted Stern as saying that 'it is the paucity of other games in the Montessori schools which makes the children take to this new occupation. In the Froebel kindergartens, with their incomparably greater variety of occupations to exercise the child's powers of intuition and imagination, his interest and independence, as a general rule, scarcely any instances of liking for reading and writing exercise are to be observed' (2).

References
(1) This quote is cited by MacNaughton in *Shaping Early Childhood* (Open University Press 2003)
(2) This quote is taken from page 255 of Smith, L *To Understand and to Help* (Associated University Presses 1985)

Where to find out more
Early Childhood Education Tina Bruce (Hodder and Stoughton 1987)

Websites:
www.montessori.edu
www.infed.org/thinkers/et-mont.htm

Useful addresses:
Montessori St Nicholas Centre, 24 Princes Gate, London SW7 1PT. Tel: 020 7584 9987
Website: www.montessori.org.uk

Montessori Education (UK) Ltd, 21 Vineyard Hill, London SW19 7JL. Tel: 020 8946 4433.
Website: www.montessorieducationuk.org

Susan Isaacs

1885 – 1948

KEY DATES

1885	Born (Susan Fairhurst) in Bromley Cross, Lancashire
1913-14	Lecturer in psychology, Darlington Training College
1916-33	Tutor in psychology, University of London
1921	Assistant editor of the British Journal of Psychology
1922	Marries Nathan Isaacs
1924-27	Principal of Malting House School, Cambridge
1933-43	Head of Department of Child Development, University of London, Institute of Education
1948	Awarded CBE for services to education in January. Dies in October

LINKS

- Froebel
- Dewey
- Montessori
- Piaget
- Sigmund Freud and psychoanalytical theories

Her life

Susan Isaacs (nee Fairhurst) was born in the village of Bromley Cross near Bolton in Lancashire in 1885. She was the ninth child of William and Miriam Fairhurst. Her father was a lay preacher in the Methodist church as well as a journalist. Her mother became ill shortly after the birth of her last child, Alice, and died when Susan was six years old. Her father had employed a nurse to care for his wife during her long illness and after his wife's death he married her.

As she was growing up, Susan Isaacs was particularly influenced by her brother, Enoch, who introduced her to philosophy. She became agnostic which led to a rift between her and her father for some years, and she also became interested in music and politics.

She left school early - before she was fifteen – and became a nursery governess abroad. She then returned to work in a small private school in Bolton but soon realised that she would not get far without formal training.

Isaacs persuaded her father to allow her to take a training course for non-graduates, but her tutors recognised her ability and asked her to consider taking a degree. To be eligible, she had to learn Greek and German, which she managed in just three months. Her father died during her first year on the course.

Isaacs gained a first class honours degree in philosophy at Manchester. This won her a post-graduate scholarship at Newnham College, Cambridge, where she studied psychology.

Her first job was as a lecturer in infant education at Darlington Training College. During this time she married a former fellow student at Manchester, William Brierley, a botanist. The marriage was dissolved after five years.

In 1922, she married Nathan Isaacs, who was ten years younger than her. She began her medical training to become a psychoanalyst and passed her preliminary examinations. She became associated with the work of the National Institute of Industrial Psychology and the British Psychological Society, writing the book Introduction to Psychology.

Educational experiment

In 1924 Isaacs responded to a newspaper advertisement for someone to set up an educational experiment. Geoffrey Pyke and his wife, Margaret, wanted to establish a small school, catering for up to 20 children, where new teaching ideas could be tried. Isaacs was employed to set up and run the school, which was for children from two and a half to seven. One of the pupils was David Pyke, the only son of Geoffrey and Margaret.

The Malting House School, as it was called, put the emphasis on children's curiosity, their emotional needs and on the importance of language. It attracted many critics as well as interest in its liberal educational ideas.

Geoffrey Pyke wanted to teach his son himself but his travels made that impractical. He believed children's minds should be set free so they could observe and draw their own conclusions. He believed in learning through discovery rather than adult-led instruction. His friend, Professor John Cohen, quotes Pyke as saying (1):
'The fundamental principle we should follow in dealing with children is to treat every child as a distinguished foreign visitor who knows little or nothing of our language or customs. If we invited a distinguished stranger to tea and he spilled his cup on the best table cloth or consumed more than his share of cake, we should not upbraid him and send him out of the room. We should hasten to reassure him that all was well. One rude remark from the host would drive the visitor

With the outbreak of war in 1939, Susan Isaacs became involved once more with children. She moved back to Cambridge and started work on a research project studying 86 evacuees and their carers. The work was later published in 1941 as The Cambridge Evacuation Survey.

Two more of her books were published: Childhood and After, a collection of papers, and Troubles of Children and Parents. In January 1948 she was awarded the CBE for her services to education. She died in October that year.

Her writing

Susan Isaacs began her writing career in 1916 with an article in a journal called Parents' Review. Over the next 30 years she wrote many papers and books for academic audiences, but she also wrote for parents. She wrote books for lay audiences as well as a column for parents in Nursery World from 1929 to 1936, under the pen-name of Ursula Wise. Much of her work drew on her experiences at Malting House, where she had kept detailed records and observations.

Some of her best known publications include:

Books for parents
▪ *The Nursery Years* (Routledge 1929)
▪ *The Children We Teach* (University of London Press 1932)

Books based on the Malting House School Study
▪ *Intellectual Growth in Young Children* (Routledge 1930)
▪ *Social Development of Young Children* (Routledge 1933)

Studies based on further practical work
▪ *The Educational Guidance of the School Child* (1936)
▪ *The Cambridge Evacuation Survey* (1941)

Her theory

Observation was the cornerstone of Isaacs' work with children. It allowed her to reflect on children's learning. Everything that happened was recorded in meticulous detail.

She believed that free, unfettered play was of great importance to young children. She wrote (2):

'Through play... he (sic) adds to his knowledge of the world...... No experimental scientist has a greater thirst for new facts than an ordinary healthy active child.

'Not all his play, however is directed to exploring the physical world or practising new skills. Much of it is social in direction, and belongs to the world of phantasy. He plays at being father and mother, the new baby sister, the policeman, the soldier; at going for a journey, at going to bed and getting up, and all the things

from the room, never to be seen again. But we address children constantly in the rudest fashion and yet expect them to behave as models of politeness. If the principle suggested is to prove effective, there must be no exceptions. One rude remark to the child would give the game away.'

Children's emotional needs

Susan Isaacs believed in the importance of play and that, with gentle guidance, children could make sense of the world for themselves. She was especially sensitive to the emotional needs of children and taught that adults should never be sarcastic towards children, or break promises made to them. Children's fantasies should not be curbed and their questions should be answered seriously and respectfully.

Isaacs stayed at the school for four years and spent the next few years writing up her observations and records. She became attached to her pupils and maintained an interest in them for many years. There are suggestions that she left the Malting House when money became an issue and that she disagreed with Pyke's idiosyncratic views on language development.

Her books, Intellectual Growth in Young Children and Social Development of Young Children, were both based on her work at the Malting House School. The first describes in detail every aspect of the school. Its aims were to stimulate curiosity rather than teach a curriculum. The Children We Teach and The Nursery Years, which is considered to be her best work, were also based on her experience at Malting House.

Six years later Isaacs was appointed head of the new Department of Child Development at the University of London's Institute of Education. In 1935, Isaacs was diagnosed with cancer but she continued to work.

Putting the theory into practice

Evelyn Lawrence, a contemporary of Susan Isaacs, identifies the three most interesting things about Malting House School as:

- the emphasis on curiosity and finding out;
- the use and development of language to promote thinking; and
- the attention paid to children's emotional needs.

The school room opened onto a garden, where there was a summer house, sand pit, see-saw (built to Pyke's design) and hutches for rabbits. Each child had a little plot to cultivate and there were fruit trees. The school had the first climbing frame seen in this country. Children were allowed to use double-handed tree saws to encourage co-operation and a range of other tools were available.

Inside, there was a piano, a rest gallery with mattresses and rugs, huge amounts of art and craft materials, easels and small tables and chairs (a legacy of the influence of Maria Montessori). There was a real typewriter - and every imaginable kind of equipment from dressing-up clothes to magnifying glasses.

The equipment enabled children to follow their interests and Isaacs also encouraged children's curiosity to be rooted in real life. Where interests demanded posting letters, additional purchases or visits, these activities became part of the children's experiences. There was no fixed curriculum - children followed their interests. There were few rules and no punishments.

Evelyn Lawrence describes the happiness of the children as her first impression of the Malting House School: 'I have never seen so much pleased concentration, so many shrieks and gurgles and jumpings for joy as here' (4).

Lawrence saw advantages for children in the free environment which Isaacs created. She said that it allowed adults to really get to know children, that their emotions were not hidden and that children learned to regulate their own behaviour within the social group, rather than relying on adults to make decisions for them.

Her influence

Isaacs' writings had a huge impact on the educational world of the late 1920s and 1930s. Isaacs said that her ideas were based on those of Froebel and Dewey but she made those ideas accessible in the way she interpreted and explained them. The combination of curricular ideas with psychoanalytical influences made a major contribution to this field.

The rigour which she brought to her work at the institute gave early childhood education a place in academic circles. She visited Piaget's research centre in Geneva and hosted his visit to the Malting House School in 1927. She was critical of some

which he sees grown-ups doing. Here also his play makes it easier for him to fit himself into his social world. When he becomes the father and the mother, he wins an imaginative insight into their attitude to him, and some little understanding of their sayings and doings; and momentarily feels their powers and great gifts (as they seem to him) as his own. All the things he may not do and cannot be in real life, he is able to do and be in this play world...'

Susan Isaacs' interest in psychoanalysis led her to explore the importance of children's emotional development. Together with Cyril Burt (whose work on intelligence testing was well respected in the 1930s but subsequently discredited) she gave evidence for the government Report on Infant and Nursery Schools in 1933. This extract from their evidence (3) gives a flavour of the kind of nursery Susan Isaacs believed best supported young children's development:

'Quiet, positive encouragement, showing the child what to do and how to do it, is far more effective than scolding or punishment, or emphasis on what he (sic) should not do. Successes should be emphasised; failures should be minimised; and above all any feeling of shame or hostility should be avoided.'

Isaacs' philosophy was based on Froebel's notion of learning by doing and inspired by John Dewey's ideas about social interaction and supporting children's interests. The Malting House School exemplified Dewey's belief that education is about living and not simply a preparation for it.

of Piaget's work, believing that he placed too little emphasis on the social and emotional aspects of learning. She disagreed with his view of children's development as a staged process. For her, children's development differed from adults only in the amount of experience that they had to draw on.

Comment

Isaacs' theories were based on her experiences with a small group of advantaged children. There were usually only ten children at the Malting House School at any one time. The children came from rich, academic families, were mostly boys who were considered bright and with a high incidence of difficult or challenging behaviour.

References

(1) This quote is cited on page 19 of van der Eyken, W and Turner, B (1975) *Adventures in Education* (Pelican Books)
(2) Isaacs, S (1929) *The Nursery Years* (Routledge and Kegan Paul) (page 10-11)
(3) Smith, L (1985) *To Understand and to Help: the Life and Works of Susan Isaacs* (Fairleigh Dickinson University Press) (cited by Smith, on page 58)
(4) Cited by Smith, on page 73

Where to find out more
To Understand and to Help: the Life and Works of Susan Isaacs L Smith (Fairleigh Dickinson University Press 1985)
Adventures in Education W van der Eyken and B Turner (Pelican Books 1975) (Chapter 1)

Jean Piaget

1896 – 1980

PROFILE

Jean Piaget was the Swiss expert who has dominated thought on the nature of children's thinking and learning since the 1960s.

KEY DATES

1896	Born at Neuchatel, Switzerland
1918	Becomes a Doctor of Natural Sciences
1921	Becomes Director of Studies at Jean Jacques Rousseau Institute, Geneva
1923	Marries Valentine Chatenay
1923	Becomes Professor of Psychology, Sociology and Philosophical Sciences, University of Neuchatel
1925	Daughter, Jacqueline, born
1927	Daughter, Lucienne, born
1929	Becomes Professor of Child Psychology, University of Geneva
1930	Son, Laurent, born
1933	Becomes Director of Institute for Educational Sciences, University of Geneva
1938	Becomes Director of Psychology and Sociology, University of Lausanne
1940	Becomes Director of Experimental Psychology, University of Geneva
1971	Made Professor Emeritus, University of Geneva
1980	Dies on 16 September, in Geneva

LINKS

- Isaacs
- Vygotsky
- Donaldson
- Gardner

His life

Jean Piaget was born in Neuchatel in Switzerland in August 1896. At the age of ten he published his first scientific paper - an observation of an albino sparrow he had discovered near his home.

An after-school job at the local natural history museum led him to write a series of articles on molluscs and he was invited to become a curator at a museum in Geneva. However, he declined because he wanted to continue his secondary education.

His godfather, the Swiss scholar Samuel Cornut, introduced him to philosophy and epistemology, the theory of knowledge, but Piaget chose to study zoology. He studied at the University of Neuchatel and completed his doctorate in 1918. Even at this young age, he had published articles and written a philosophical novel in which he outlined the epistemological issues that were to occupy him for life.

After graduating, Piaget became interested in psychology, which was still a new science. He went to Zurich where he studied under Carl Jung and Eugen Bleuler, then to the Sorbonne in Paris for two years.

It was here that he administered reading tests to schoolchildren and worked with Alfred Binet who was devising intelligence tests. Piaget became bored with counting the number of correct answers, but fascinated by his discovery that children of the same age often gave the same incorrect answers. This led him to explore the development of the reasoning process. His observations led him to believe that there were consistent measurable differences in the nature of reasoning at different ages.

In 1921, he returned to Switzerland where he was appointed Director of the Jean Jacques Rousseau Institute in Geneva. Two years later, Piaget married and returned to his home town of Neuchatel, becoming Professor of Psychology, Sociology and Philosophy at his old university.

Piaget observed and recorded the development of all three of his children. This shaped his understanding and theories about the ways in which children construct knowledge.

Piaget moved back to Geneva in 1929, remaining there until his death in 1980.

His writing

Piaget wrote many books and articles. In many of them, he continued the work started in Paris, developing his theory that the mind of the child evolves through a series of pre-determined stages to adulthood.

- *The Psychology of Intelligence* (Routledge Classics 2001)
  First published as La Psychologie de l'intelligence in 1947
  First published in English in 1950

- *The Language and Thought of the Child* (Routledge Classics 2002)
  First published as Le langage et la pensee chez l'enfant in 1923
  First published in English in 1926

His theory

There are five important aspects of his theories in relation to young children.

Stages of development

Piaget's contemporary, Freud, also identified staged development. While Freud focused on emotional and sexual development, Piaget was interested in intellectual development. Piaget saw the child as constantly constructing and re-constructing reality - achieving increased understanding by integrating simple concepts into more complex ones at each stage of development. He argued that there was a natural sequence for the development of thought governed by what he termed 'genetic epistemology'. It was not enough to teach ideas by simple reinforcement or practice - the child had to be at a particular stage of development to be able to learn new concepts.

Piaget identified four stages in that process, from birth through to adulthood:

Sensorimotor stage

Piaget described the first two years of a child's life as the sensorimotor stage when babies' and toddlers' knowledge and understanding are chiefly drawn from physical action and their senses - sight, sound, taste, touch and smell. He suggested that throughout this stage children remain egocentric but become aware of object permanence (see below).

Preoperational stage

From the age of two to around six or seven years of age, children learn to manipulate the environment and to represent objects by words, which supports play with ideas. Logic rests on incomplete knowledge - children of this age may, for example, explain the wind by claiming that trees make it.

Concrete operational stage

In the third stage, from about seven to eleven years of age, logical thought develops, with the child emphasising classification or categorisation by similarity and difference. Logic is normally only applied to things that are tangible or can be seen.

Formal operations stage

The fourth and final stage begins at around the age of twelve and continues through into adulthood. Piaget claimed that this stage was characterised by orderly thinking and mastery of logical thought. Children can manipulate abstract ideas, make hypotheses and see the implications of their thinking and that of others.

Equilibrium, accommodation and assimilation

One of Piaget's many ideas is auto-regulation or equilibrium. When we take in new information - through the feel of something, sounds, sights or smells - in Piaget's terms we assimilate the information. We are aware of the new sensation or experience but simply put the information alongside our existing ideas. Sooner or later something happens which causes us to call our new idea into question, we experience some discomfort or disequilibrium which causes us to rethink the idea we had assimilated. The rethinking is known as accommodation - we have to adjust or re-organise our thinking in order to restore equilibrium - feeling comfortable with our thinking.

An example of this might be when a young child picks up a piece of paper and the toy which was wrapped up inside it falls out, making a sound. The baby will at first assimilate the idea that paper makes a clunking sound - testing out the idea on several pieces of paper. Over time he or she begins to realise that not all paper makes that particular sound, disequilibrium follows and will lead to an accommodation of the view that paper can only produce that particular sound in certain circumstances.

Piaget used the term schema to describe the mental representations that develop as children have new experiences and put new ideas and abilities together. This term was later used by Chris Athey (see pages 50-51). It has many meanings but during the past 20 years has come to have a specific meaning in the education of young children.

Object permanence

Piaget watched his daughter, Jacqueline, at the age of seven months trying to catch a toy duck on her quilt. She reached to grasp the toy but it slid away from her between the folds. Although she followed the movement with her eyes, as soon as the duck disappeared, she no longer looked for it. Some months later, Piaget put a coin in his hand and hid his hand under the bed cover. When he pulled his hand out from under the cover, his daughter opened it to find the coin. Because it was not there she immediately looked under the cover and found it. These observations led to the formation of Piaget's theory of object permanence - the realisation that objects have their own existence, independent of our perception of them.

Egocentrism

After observing his own children, Piaget carried out a series of experiments with young children. In one of the experiments, he showed children in the pre-operational stage of development a model of three distinctive mountains. A small doll was moved about on the model. Children were shown a series of photographs of the mountains and asked to identify which of the pictures showed what the doll would be able to see from various viewpoints. Most of the children were unable to select the appropriate photograph, choosing instead the one which gave their own point of view. Piaget described this as egocentrism.

Conservation

Piaget also carried out a series of conservation task experiments with children under seven years of age. In these experiments, children might be presented with two balls of Plasticene weighing the same. One ball would be flattened and the children asked to predict whether the two lumps would now weigh the same or different. Similarly they might be presented with two identical short, fat beakers of liquid. One would be poured into a tall thin container and, again, children would be asked to say whether the two amounts of liquid were still the same or whether they were different. In another, similar experiment two rows of buttons were compared before and after one row had been spread out so that it was longer.

Jean Piaget

In these experiments, younger children tended to assume that the amounts had changed, while as they grew older they realised that the amounts stayed the same, whether or not their visual perception supported this view.

Putting the theory into practice

Piaget's theories have practical implications:

- New ideas and knowledge should be presented at a level and style consistent with the child's current mode of thought. Piaget suggested that there were limitations to the logical thought of young children.
- Teaching should be matched to the needs of individuals. Children should be presented with moderately novel situations or experiences to trigger assimilation and accommodation. Open-ended questions can support this process.
- Learning is supported by action. Children need to experiment actively with materials and to experience things in the real world to develop thought.
- Children need to have control over their learning - learning how to find out and constructing knowledge for themselves. This requires open-ended activities.
- Children require long, uninterrupted periods of play and exploration.
- Observation of what children do and say can and should inform understanding of children's intellectual development – this will tell us where they need support.

His influence

Piaget's theories dominated developmental psychology in the 1960s and 70s. His theories were covered in teacher training and were influential in the education of young children.

Many theorists – such as Susan Isaacs, Jerome Bruner and Margaret Donaldson - studied with him over many decades and his influence continues to be felt. Seymour Papert (who developed the computer language, Logo) described Piaget as having 'found the secrets of human learning and knowledge hidden behind the cute and seemingly illogical notions of children' while Albert Einstein said that Piaget's work was 'a discovery so simple that only a genius could have thought of it' (1).

Comment

Piaget is said to be one of the most frequently mentioned and least understood developmental psychologists. His major achievements were in creating a sense of curiosity about the ways in which children learn - his interest was primarily in how children learn as opposed to what or when they might learn it.

Criticisms of his work include:

- Too much emphasis on logic and mathematical thinking.
- The findings from both the observations of his own children and his experiments are over-generalised from a narrow range of subjects.
- The stages offer a snapshot of development. Observations could be interpreted to show continuous development as opposed to the shifts in thinking which Piaget described.
- Insufficient emphasis on the importance of social and emotional aspects of thought.
- Some experiments have shown that when what we ask children to do, or respond to, makes 'human sense' (2) - they are able to take another's point of view and to conserve quantities. When a naughty child hiding from a policeman is substituted for mountains or when a naughty teddy bear spreads out the row of buttons, children are more likely to give the correct answers.

References
(1) Both quotes are taken from the website www.time.com/time/time100/scientist/profile/piaget.html
(2) Donaldson, M (1978) *Children's Minds* (Fontana)

Where to find out more
Extending Thought in Young Children Chris Athey (Paul Chapman Publishing 1990)
How the Child's Mind Develops D Cohen (Routledge 2002)
Theories of Childhood: an Introduction to Dewey, Montessori, Erikson, Piaget and Vygotsky C G Mooney (Redleaf Press 2000)

Website:
www.time.com/time/time100/scientist/profile/piaget.html

Lev Vygotsky

His life

Lev Vygotsky was born in 1896 in Orscha, Belarus. His family were middle-class Jews - his father a bank manager and local philanthropist. As a child, he studied with a private tutor for many years until he was enrolled in a Jewish grammar school which prepared pupils for entrance to university.

As a teenager, Vygotsky was an intellectual with a wide range of interests, especially in philosophy and history, including Jewish culture. He graduated from school with honours. At his parents' insistence he applied to the Medical School of Moscow University. Only three per cent of the university's intake were Jewish and places were allocated through a draw. Vygotsky gained a place and was at the university from 1913 to 1917. He switched from medicine to law during his first term.

At the same time, he enrolled at the private Shaniavsky University where he studied history, literature and philosophy. He became interested in a wide range of subjects, including the theatre and was an aspiring literary critic. After graduating, Vygotsky went to Gomel, where his parents lived, and took a job teaching literature in the provincial school. It was there that his health began to deteriorate. He was 23.

The school did not suit his ambitions but he soon found a job at a local teachers' training college where he lectured in psychology and became involved in the education of children with physical disabilities.

In 1924, at the second Psychoneural Congress in Leningrad, Vygotsky gave a talk on the relationship between conditioned reflexes and the conscious behaviour of humans. His work so impressed his audience that, at the age of 28, Vygotsky was invited to become a research fellow at the Moscow Institute of Psychology.

During his time in Moscow, Vygotsky wrote about 100 books and papers. He read and reflected on the work of Freud and Piaget. He travelled in Europe during the 1920s and was influenced by a range of writers, including Charlotte Buhler who studied the development of language in babies and children.

Vygotsky was also involved in applied research. His experimental studies in educational psychology were developed in his work with mentally and physically disabled children and more generally in the field of psychopathology.

Lev Vygotsky was a Soviet psychologist whose book, Thought and Language, has become a classic text in university courses on psycholinguistics. He is best known for his emphasis on the way in which children's cultural and social context influences their development. Although he died young and his work was not translated into English until the second half of the twentieth century, he has had a strong influence on the development of current educational theories.

KEY DATES

1896	Born in Orscha, Belarus
1913-1917	Moscow University
1924	Research fellow, Moscow Institute of Psychology
1925	Writes *The Psychology of Art* (not published until 1965, translated into English in 1971)
1926	Writes *The Historical Meaning of the Crisis in Psychology* (published in 1982)
1931	Finishes writing *History of the Development of Higher Mental Functions* (published in 1983)
1934	Dies

His writing

Vygotsky was a prolific writer. Much of his work has not been translated into English but some books have been published in a range of translations and editions. His best known or most influential are:

- *Thought and Language* (published in 1962 by MIT Press)
- *Mind in Society* (published in 1978 by Harvard University Press, edited by M Cole et al)

His theory

Language and thinking

Vygotsky emphasised the significant role that language plays in the development of abstract thought. He stressed the importance of the labelling process in the formulation of concepts. He believed that children's language was social in origin because it arose in interaction between the child and others. In other words, the child's language both results from and is part of social interaction.

He saw the experience of talking with adults about familiar everyday experiences as crucial, not only for building up knowledge of language but also for an awareness of particular ways of thinking and interpreting their own experiences. The very naming of particular attributes, he thought, helped concepts to form. This contrasts with Piaget's view that the use of relevant language follows the development of a concept.

Vygotsky believed that talking is necessary to clarify important points but also that talking with others helps us to learn more about communication. Children solve practical tasks with the help of speech, as well as with their eyes and hands. The idea that children observe conversation and that it is the unity of perception, speech and action which leads them to make sense of situations was important in Vygotsky's thinking. Children do not simply react to the words that are used but interpret the context, facial expression, and body language to understand meaning.

Young children also talk to themselves. They use language as a tool for regulating or guiding their actions. An example of this might be the toddler declaring 'up step' as they climb a flight of stairs or a four-year-old creating a story as they draw or paint. Language usually becomes internalised by the age of seven, except where tasks are difficult – adults often talk to themselves through a difficult task or read instructions out loud.

The zone of proximal development

Vygotsky also developed a theory called the 'zone of proximal development' which he described as the gap between what a child can do alone and what they can do with the help of someone more skilled or experienced, who could be an adult or another child.

He argued that the capacity to learn through instruction was a fundamental feature of human intelligence. Where adults help a child to learn, they are fostering the development of knowledge and ability. Piaget believed that learning was dependent on the child's readiness to learn. For Vygotsky, the key factors were not only the child's existing knowledge or understanding but also their ability to learn with help. Two children may have similar levels of competence but different levels of success because of their differing abilities to benefit from the help or instruction given them by adults. For this reason, he objected to measuring children's abilities through intelligence tests, believing that what could be observed about how the child went about a task could reveal as much as the score of any test.

Vygotsky rated children's interaction between themselves as important. In his view, interaction benefits a child when they are helped by another child who knows more about the task. The more knowledgeable child benefits too, as the process of making their ideas more explicit renders the grasp of what they know clearer and more objective.

The social context for learning

For Vygotsky social and cognitive development work together. While Piaget believed that knowledge comes from personal experience, Vygotsky emphasised the importance of families, communities and other children.

Vygotsky saw language as one of a range of cultural tools or tools for thinking which we learn from others and use with others in thinking and learning. Other such tools are numbers, signs, notations, plans and diagrams. He also thought that play and imagination were important to development and learning.

Putting the theory into practice

The notion of the zone of proximal development emphasises the importance of what has been called 'scaffolding'. This relies on careful observation of what children can do and planning a curriculum which challenges their current capability.

Like Piaget, Vygotsky emphasised the way in which knowledge and understanding are constructed by the learner from their experiences. This is known as constructivist theory. Unlike Piaget, however, who saw experience as personal, Vygotsky emphasised the social components of experience. His theory underlined the contribution to learning made by others, and is known as a social constructivist view. It has been associated with an apprenticeship approach where the learner learns from someone more experienced or competent. Key ideas in a classroom then become conversation, play and opportunities to follow interests and ideas.

His influence

Vygotsky's concept of differing zones of proximal development led to important new techniques for diagnosing children's learning needs and

the development of teaching techniques to meet them.

The idea of matching tasks to children's current competence to scaffold their learning comes directly from his work. His theories changed the way educators think about children's interactions with others, and led to peer tutoring approaches and to apprenticeship views of learning. Schemes encouraging children to read at home with their parents rely on a view that children are apprentice readers.

Vygotsky's ideas balance those of Piaget and helped others build on and develop new theories from those of Piaget. The work of Bruner, for example, owes much to Vygotsky. American psychologist Barbara Rogoff (1) has developed theories based on Vygotsky's emphasis on culture and society.

Comment

Because Vygotsky died so young, criticisms of his work have not been as detailed or as analytical as those of Piaget's work. His work was not widely known outside Russia for many years after his death.

In emphasising the nurture side of learning (the impact of others and the scaffolding they offer to learning), it could be argued that there is not enough emphasis on children's role in their own development – the nature of learning, the role played by the developmental process and the child's own personality.

The second criticism concerns Vygotsky's methodologies. Much of his work was not based on empirical evidence but were untested ideas or hypotheses.

References
See for example:
Rogoff, B *Apprenticeship in Thinking* (Oxford University Press 1990) and *The Cultural Nature of Human Development* (Oxford University Press 2003)

Where to find out more
Theories of Childhood: an Introduction to Dewey, Montessori, Erikson, Piaget and Vygotsky C G Mooney (Redleaf Press 2000)

Burrhus Skinner

1904 – 1990

PROFILE

Burrhus Skinner is probably the best known behaviourist theorist. Skinner applied ideas taken from his work with rats and pigeons to children. His approach is called operant conditioning. He was identified in a 1975 survey as the best-known American scientist of his day.

KEY DATES

1904   Born in Pennsylvania, USA

1990   Dies

LINKS

▪ Bandura offered a link between behaviourism and cognitive psychology, found in the theories of Piaget and Vygotsky.

His life

Burrhus Skinner was born in 1904 in Pennsylvania, USA. At university, he had aspirations to be a writer. He wrote poetry, took courses in Greek, creative writing and drama and became editor of the student newspaper. He also enjoyed painting and music. After graduating, Skinner wrote to the poet, Robert Frost, asking for advice about a career. Frost's response led him to apply for a course in psychology at Harvard University. In the late 1920s, Skinner read the work of Ivan Pavlov and John Watson. Their theories later influenced his work.

His writing

Skinner has had many books and articles in journals published, from early in his career until he was more than 80 years old. These are some of his more famous works:

▪ *The Behaviour of Organisms: an experimental analysis* (Prentice Hall 1938)

Behaviourism

Behavourist theories began with the work of **Ivan Pavlov (1849-1936)** who used classical conditioning. He discovered that dogs could be trained (or conditioned) to salivate when a bell rang, if feeding was consistently preceded by a bell ringing. Salivating at the sight of food when hungry is a natural response - by pairing a natural response with an artificial one the two become associated with one another. The response is conditioned.

Edward Thorndike (1874-1949) was a leading educational psychologist in the USA throughout the first half of the twentieth century. He developed the law of effect which suggests that any behaviour leading to a positive consequence will be repeated. Through his experiments with animals he found that repetition improved the ability to solve problems.

Around the same time, **John Watson (1878-1954)** was suggesting that operant conditioning is concerned with controlling actions by providing a stimulus after rather than before the action. When reinforcement follows a behaviour, that behaviour is likely to be repeated. In other words, if an adult says 'well done' or gives a child a sweet every time they eat everything on their dinner plate, the child will continue to clear their plate at mealtimes.

Watson (1) famously believed that he could shape any child's development saying: 'Give me a dozen healthy infants, well-formed, and my own specified world to bring them up in, and I'll guarantee to take anyone at random and train him to become any type of specialist I might select - doctor, lawyer, artist, merchant-chief, and yes even beggar-man and thief, regardless of his talents, penchants, tendencies, abilities, vocations, and race of his ancestors.'

Albert Bandura (1925 -), a Canadian, is known as the father of cognitivists. His social learning theory built on behaviourist theories. Bandura's work started as a study of aggression in adolescents, sometimes known as the 'bobo doll studies'. He claimed that aggressive behaviour was learned through observing and imitating role models. Bandura's view is that learning occurs as a result of stimulus (such as the bell) and response (salivating) or the promise of sweets and a clean dinner plate. He claims, however, that the reinforcement occurs as a result of our observation and imitation of other humans, as we try to be like others we like or admire. MacNaughton (2) explains Bandura's work on social learning theory as follows: 'Children frequently learn, through observation, the behaviour of both sexes, however, they usually perform only the behaviour appropriate to their own sex because this is what they have been reinforced to do'.

Bandura's theory has acted as a bridge between behaviourism and developmental theories. Like behaviourism, it takes account of the mind, or mental dimensions of human learning, but also recognises that reinforcement is not always immediate and that learning may occur where there is no immediate or apparent reward.

Burrhus Skinner

- 'The science of learning and the art of teaching' Harvard Educational Review 24: 86-97 (1954)
- *Verbal Behaviour* (Appleton-Century-Crofts 1957)
- 'Teaching machines' *Scientific American* November 1961, pages 91-102
- *Beyond Freedom and Dignity* (Alfred Knopf 1971)

His theory

Skinner conducted most of his experiments on rodents and pigeons but wrote most of his books about people. To him, people and animals are organisms – differing only in the degree of sophistication they bring to a learning situation.

Behaviourism is sometimes known as learning theory. Learning and development are often portrayed in terms of nature versus nurture. Behaviourism is at the extreme nurture end of this debate - behaviourists generally believe that all behaviour is learned and that it can be shaped.

The popular view is that behaviour is shaped by punishment and rewards – that humans act to avoid punishment and gain reward. Skinner emphasised reward. He believed that punishment was counter-productive. He broke tasks down into small steps, each step reinforced and rewarded as it was learned. Although Skinner's experiments were generally carried out on animals, his work became widely applied to child development and to work with parents.

Putting the theory into practice

Behaviourist theory is responsible for teaching methods which focus on the repetition of words and on completing row upon row of sums. Programmed instruction was launched in the 1950s with materials presented in small steps.

Behaviourism is most often seen in the teaching of children with special educational needs and in behaviour management. Breaking tasks down into small steps; star charts rewarding children for keeping to rules; withdrawal of privileges when children do not keep to rules – these approaches all come from behaviourism. Similar techniques are often applied to persistently crying babies – the advice is not to pick babies up when they cry as this will reinforce the crying behaviour.

His influence

Skinner also applied behaviourism to language. He believed that all language was learned by reward – for example, when the baby says 'da-da-da' we praise them, but we don't reinforce sounds that we don't recognise or link to other words.

Noam Chomsky, an American professor of linguistics, was so opposed to Skinner's views that he developed a theory, based on the idea of language development as an innate process. He hypothesised that we are born with a 'language acquisition device' which gives us an inbuilt understanding of language structures. Chomsky's argument, spurred by Skinner's view,

stimulated experiment and thinking about language throughout the second half of the twentieth century.

Social learning theory has played a role in making practitioners aware of children's need to:

- be offered positive role models in behaviour and conflict resolution, and in habits such as reading and healthy eating;
- observe and therefore practise behaviours;
- build strong and positive relationships.

Comment

The philosopher Arthur Koestler said 'For the anthropomorphic view of the rat, American psychology substituted a rattomorphic view of man' (3). This is the most common criticism of behaviourism, that since it focused on animals it is too simplistic a view of human learning and motivation. Rewards can become counter-productive. Studies in which young children were rewarded for drawing pictures, for example, demonstrated that quickly children no longer drew pictures unless they were rewarded.

Behaviourism ignores the emotional states and complex motives that account for human behaviour. Humans are treated as though they lack mind or soul and consist only of a brain that responds to external stimuli.

It does not explain many phenomena in learning. Language learning in young children is a good example of something that cannot be explained through stimulus-response approaches. Small children say things that they have never heard – they make up words, merge words, overgeneralise rules, and so on. They may also fail to say things for which they are rewarded – such as please and thank you! It ignores, too, the way in which patterns of learning can be adapted to new information and the role of thoughtful judgement and reflection in human thinking.

References

(1) Keenan, T (2002) *An Introduction to Child Development* (Sage) (Keenan quotes Watson on page 11)
(2) MacNaughton, G (2003) *Shaping Early Childhood* (Open University Press) (On page 32 MacNaughton cites Crain)
(3) Kohn, A (1993) Punished by *Rewards* (Houghton Mifflin)

Where to find out more
Fifty Modern Thinkers on Education J Palmer (Routledge 2001)

John Bowlby

PROFILE

John Bowlby's theory of attachment argued that a child's emotional bond to their familial caregiver was a biological response that ensured survival. The quality of attachment, he said, has implications for the child's capacity to form trusting relationships.

KEY DATES

1907   Born

1969   *Attachment and Loss* (Vol 1: Attachment) is published

1990   Dies

LINKS

- Emotional intelligence (see pages 79-80)
- Psychoanalysis (see pages 17-22)

His life

After the Second World War, the psychiatrist John Bowlby was commissioned by the World Health Organisation (WHO) to study the mental health needs of homeless and orphaned children. In his report, Maternal Care and Mental Health, he documented the depth of distress in the children he had seen. In his view, this distress could not be explained by the main theories of the time.

One of these theories explained the distress as a kind of 'cupboard love'. To meet their physical needs for food, warmth and protection, children attached themselves to an adult who would provide them. This attachment was secondary to the main purpose of sustenance and protection. However, the depth and manner of young children's responses to separation from adults seemed to Bowlby to go beyond this.

In trying to reach a new understanding of these relationships, he turned to the work of a number of other researchers. One was James Robertson, a psychiatric social worker, who had recorded on film the reactions of young children in short separations from their parents. The children's distress and withdrawal evident in these films had a big impact on public and professional debate about the impact of separation on young children. Another was Harry Harlow, an American scientist studying the interactions between rhesus monkeys and their mothers. Harlow found that, when frightened, baby monkeys preferred a comforting mother to a feeding mother. These monkeys were demonstrating that attachment to the 'maternal monkey' mattered in its own right for the sense of comfort and security it provided.

Bowlby continued to study how children bond with adults, and their reaction to separation from adults, over the 20 years that followed the publication of the WHO report. In 1969 he published his first book about attachment theory.

His writing

- *Child Care and the Growth of Love* (Penguin 1965)
- *Attachment and Loss Vol 1: Attachment* (Penguin 1969)
- *Attachment and Loss Vol 2: Separation* (Penguin 1973)

His theory

Attachment theory has developed and evolved since Bowlby first wrote about it, but the striking features remain:

- Children show a marked preference for closeness to a small number of adults and these attachments are a normal and universal part of human development.
- Babies are born adapted to seek out such attachments not primarily with the aim of being fed and protected but for the feelings of safety and security the attachment brings.
- The particular attachment between infant and adult is formed as an interaction in which both play a part.
- Attachment behaviour, that is the actions of the infant to bring about physical closeness with an attachment figure, increases when the infant feels frightened or anxious and decreases when the infant feels safe and secure.
- As infants mature into adulthood, the need for attachment figures lessens; however, attachment behaviour continues across the life cycle and we find ourselves returning to seek comfort or reassurance from loved ones in times of stress or anxiety.
- Our experiences of attachment in infancy, that is how well and how reliably adults respond to infants' feelings of anxiety and dread and expressions of love, influence our closest relationships throughout life.

There is a sensitive period of some two years for forming these earliest attachments but if early relationships are disrupted, for whatever reason, many other factors come into play to determine how children cope and develop - resilience depends on much more than just the first two years.

Putting the theory into practice

The attachment theory was a convenient idea for post-war politicians. During the war women had done jobs that were now needed for men returning from the war. Many local authorities developed policies that children under the age of three should be at home with their mothers. If parents wanted day care for their children then it should be with childminders not nurseries.

Nurseries for children over three that had provided full-time places during the war, now only took children part-time. It was argued that this made more places available but also that children of this age benefited from being at home with their mothers.

The main positive outcomes of good attachment experiences in the early years seem to be social ones:

- self-confidence;
- efficacy;
- self-esteem;
- the capacity to care for others and to be cared for.

These attributes are associated with mastery - the disposition to believe something can be achieved and to keep on trying.

Nurseries which value the importance of children's attachments - at home and at nursery - are likely to be ones where links between home and nursery are strong; where children feel that they are known and understood; and where staff know in detail about children's interests and activities.

Many professional staff worry about children becoming too attached to them for fear it will undermine relationships at home. They don't want to set children up for painful feelings of loss when they have to leave nursery or move up a class. They also think that it may lead to favouritism.

But children can cope with several close attachments. Attachment is not a fixed quantity in children's lives. More at nursery does not mean less at home. Professional staff, supported by colleagues and managers, are well able to allow children to become attached but to maintain professional boundaries, too. Favouritism is not an inevitable consequence of closeness.

His influence

John Bowlby's work contributed to changes in services for children. After the war, many nurseries cut their hours to part-time. This had the effect of both doubling the number of available places to cater for the boom in

births as fathers returned from the war and reducing the number of women seeking employment, creating more job opportunities for men. It became increasingly difficult to obtain full day care for young children.

The work of the Robertsons – Bowlby's students - shocked the nation. (They produced the film showing the effects of separation from parents on children when hospitalised.) It was instrumental in making it possible for parents to stay in hospital with their children.

Bowlby's work led other researchers to try to assess the strength of infants' attachments to adults, mainly their mothers. Mary Ainsworth (1913-1999) pioneered this work, devising a test to see how infants of around a year old reacted in different kinds of unusual situation.

The test involved a series of short events, starting with the mother and infant settled together in a playroom. The mother left but returned in two or three minutes. The extent to which the infant became anxious at his mother's departure and how quickly and easily she was able to reassure him on her return were taken as measures of the security of his attachment to her.

Ainsworth found that most infants seemed to fall into one of two main groups. About two thirds (regarded as 'secure') were easily reassured by the return of their mother and after seeking and receiving a hug or cuddle, were happy to carry on playing. The remaining third reacted in two ways. Some became distressed when their mother departed but seemed not to want her attention when she came back, perhaps even seeming to prefer the stranger (labelled as 'anxious avoidant'). The others, when their mother returned, seemed not to know what they wanted - first seeking reassurance and then rejecting it. These were labelled as 'anxious-ambivalent'.

These classifications of attachment have gradually been refined. However, provided family circumstances remain the same, they do seem to hold steady over time. The proportions within each category seem to vary between nationalities and cultural groups.

Comment

Bowlby's work was carried out with a section of the population who had been in a severely deprived environment yet it was generalised to all children. More recent work on the importance of emotional development has caused many theorists and practitioners to reassess Bowlby's work.

Mary Ainsworth's work has been criticised as (1) failing to take account of cultural differences, acting as though cultural groups which did not match the responses of American children were somehow failing to attach appropriately.

Reference
(1) Singer, E 'Shared care for children' in Woodhead, M et al *Cultural Worlds of Early Childhood* (Routledge in conjunction with the Open University 1998)

Where to find out more
Key Times for Play J Manning-Morton and M Thorp (Open University Press 2003)

Jerome Bruner

PROFILE

Jerome Bruner is a cognitive and developmental psychologist who has been influential in education, bringing together the work of Vygotsky, Freud and Piaget. Some dissatisfaction with his own early work has led him to focus on the importance of culture in learning.

KEY DATES

1915	Born in New York City, USA
1959	Chairs joint conference of the National Academy of Sciences and the National Science Foundation in Massachusetts
1966	Publishes findings of a study investigating modes of representation used by children
1970	Joins Oxford University
1980	*Oxford Pre-School Research* is published

LINKS

- Donaldson
- Gardner
- Vygotsky

His life

Bruner's career encompasses work in many different areas of psychology. In 1959 he chaired a prestigious meeting of scientists, psychologists and educators who wanted to improve the quality of scientific education in the USA. The arguments which emerged formed the basis of Bruner's book The Process of Education and included ideas (1) which run throughout his work:

- 'Knowing how something is put together is worth a thousand facts about it.'
- The child is an active learner and problem-solver, struggling to make sense of the world.
- Intellectual activity is anywhere and everywhere – children are always learning.
- The spiral curriculum, described in Bruner's words (2) as 'any subject can be taught effectively in some intellectually honest form to any child at any stage of development'.

Bruner spent some time at Oxford University and led the Oxford Pre-School Research project in the 1980s. He was critical of some aspects of early childhood provision in this country. In the late 1990s, he began to work with the pre-schools of Reggio Emilia and other Italian communities.

His work has been increasingly influenced by Vygotsky and the emphasis which he gives to the impact of culture on learning. This has led him to a continued interest in motivation, affect, creativity, intuition – all of which go beyond behaviourism.

His writing

Howard Gardner (3), a psychologist and educationist, wrote about one of Bruner's best known books as follows:

'In the late 1980s, I attended an international conference on education in Paris. One evening I found myself having dinner with half a dozen persons, representing half a dozen different nations, none of whom I had known before. As we spoke, a remarkable fact emerged. All of us had been drawn to a life in education because of our reading, years before, of psychologist Jerome Bruner's remarkable volume, The Process of Education.'

model identifies three stages or modes: the enactive mode, which involves physical action; the iconic in which one thing stands for another, as when a child uses a banana to represent a telephone; and the symbolic mode which suggests that children represent experience through a range of symbolic systems.

While for Piaget, movement between stages was a one-way process, Bruner talks of negotiation and conflict between them. The chosen mode depends on level of experience. With things which are new to us we are more likely to choose enactive modes of representation or thinking, gradually moving towards symbolic modes as we become more experienced. Each level or mode has four stages (4) which relate to how children decide on the use of rules in representing ideas in a variety of media.

Bruner developed his theory of the spiral curriculum in the 1960s when he was thinking of ways in which to reform school curricula.

In his most recent work, Bruner emphasises the importance of culture. He believes that cultural psychology is the route to understanding people's intentional behaviour. He says that education offers a test-bed for developing the discipline of cultural psychology.

Bruner has written about the role of culture in education (6):

'It is surely the case that schooling is only one small part of how a culture inducts the young into its canonical ways. Indeed schooling may even be at odds with a culture's other ways of inducting the young into the requirements of communal living. What has become increasingly clear.... is that education is not just about conventional school matters like curriculum or standards or testing. What we resolve to do in school only makes sense when considered in the broadest context of what the society intends to accomplish through its educational investment in the young. How one conceives of education, we have finally come to recognize, is a function of how one conceives of culture, and its aims, professed or otherwise...... culture shapes the mind... It provides us with the toolkit by which we construct not only our worlds but our very conception of ourselves and our powers.'

He sees education as beginning in infancy and some of his writing has focused on mother–child interactions. He has focused on the importance of the social and playful interactions between adults and babies in supporting the development of language.

Bruner attributed the book's success to the fact that it addressed the concerns of educators about the role of knowledge in an age increasingly over-burdened by knowledge and sources of information.

- *The Process of Education* (Harvard University Press 1960)
- *The Process of Education* (Harvard University Press 1977)
- This edition has a new introduction by Bruner that attempts to examine the strengths and weaknesses of the original.
- *Play: its Role in Development and Evolution* edited in conjunction with Alison Jolly and Kathy Sylva (Penguin 1976)
- *Under Five in Britain* (Grant McIntyre 1980)
- *Child's Talk: Learning to Use Language* (Oxford University Press 1983)
- *Actual Minds: Possible Worlds* (Harvard University Press 1986)

His theory

Bruner considers the full range of human capacities that are involved in teaching and learning - perception, thought, language, other symbol systems, creativity, intuition, personality and motivation.

He has developed a model for understanding the way in which children represent experiences and turn them into knowledge. His

Putting the theory into practice

Bruner attempted to put his theories into practice by creating a curriculum entitled 'Man: a course of study', based on the fundamental questions:

- What is uniquely human about human beings?

- How did they get that way?
- How could they be made more so?

The curriculum drew on the work of contemporary thinkers such as Noam Chomsky and Levi-Strauss and included issues related to communication, tools and media, the social organisation of cultures (art, myth and child-rearing practices) and focused on the Inuit and Kalahari bushmen.

This experiment was by no means wholly successful. However, the application of Bruner's theory of stages of representation can be seen in the way in which practitioners seek to enable children to represent their ideas and experiences:

- actively through play;
- iconically through building or painting; and
- symbolically through language (written and verbal) and numbers.

Since 2000, Bruner has been involved in a project called SUMIT (Schools with Success). The factors associated with success appear to include collaboration amongst staff, a focus on the arts across the curriculum and assessment embedded in meaningful activities.

His influence

Howard Gardner (5) has described Jerome Bruner as having no peers when it comes to enlarging our sense of how children learn and what educators could aspire to.

He has developed the skills of many current thinkers. Professor Kathy Sylva, from the Institute of Education, University of London, has worked with him. She is known for her involvement with the Effective Provision of Pre-school Education (EPPE) Project. So have Howard Gardner (see pages 63-66) and Margaret Donaldson (see pages 60-62). Gardner describes him as a 'communicator, model and identification figure'.

Comment

Bruner criticised his programme 'Man: a course of study' as being too elitist or intellectual and too much concerned with non-American issues. He claimed that it worked best with well-prepared teachers working with advantaged pupils and that it had an excessive focus on the learner as an individual rather than as a member of a culture or society.

The Oxford Pre-School Research was criticised by early childhood practitioners when it was published in the 1980s. This may be because Bruner appeared to not entirely understand what practitioners were aiming to do.

References
(1) Gardner, H 'Jerome S Bruner' in Palmer, J (ed) *Fifty Modern Thinkers on Education* (Routledge 2001)
(2) Bruner, J *The Process of Education* (Harvard University Press 1960) (see page 33)
(3) Gardner, H 'Jerome S Bruner' in Palmer, J (ed) *Fifty Modern Thinkers on Education* (Routledge 2001) (see page 90)
(4) Bruce, T *Early Childhood Education* (Hodder and Stoughton 1987) (Tina Bruce describes Bruner's ideas in some detail.)
(5) Gardner, H 'Jerome S Bruner' in Palmer, J (ed) *Fifty Modern Thinkers on Education* (Routledge 2001) (see page 90)
(6) Bruner, J *Culture of Education* (Harvard University Press 1996) (page ix-x)

Where to find out more
www.infed.org/thinkers/bruner.htm

Chris Athey

Her life

The term 'schema' is used in psychology and associated in particular with Piaget. Chris Athey applied the theory to the practical observation and analysis of young children's learning.

Athey was a principal lecturer for many years at the Froebel Institute. In 1973 she set up the Froebel Early Education Project which lasted for five years, researching aspects of young children's development. Tina Bruce (now a professor in early childhood studies at the University of Roehampton, based at Froebel College), worked as her research assistant, with a group that Chris Athey described as 'disadvantaged'. They observed about 20 children for two years. A control group of socio-economically advantaged children were also studied.

The project had three main aims (1):

- To produce information on the ways in which knowledge is acquired by young children at home and school.
- To provide an effective enrichment programme for children from a disadvantaged section of the community.
- To document a number of developmental sequences of behaviour from early motor behaviours to 'thought', in sufficient detail to allow professionals to evaluate the data and the usefulness of interpretation.

Children attending the research nursery were taken on regular visits, generally with their parents, to places of interest. Their subsequent play was carefully observed and analysed. The children's representation of what they had experienced might be seen in play, drawings, block play, language or movements. Athey's account of the project was published in 1990. Tina Bruce's book, Early Childhood Education, published in 1987, also identifies examples of children's schema.

Her writing

- 'Humour in Children related to Piaget's theory of intellectual development' in Chapman, A and Foot, H (eds) It's a Funny Thing, Humour (Pergamon Press 1977)
- 'Parental Involvement in nursery education' Early Childhood Development and Care 7: 4 (1981)
- Extending Thought in Young Children (Paul Chapman Publishing 1990)

Her theory

For Chris Athey (2) there are many different definitions of schema but no single one on which everyone would agree. She suggests that in Piaget's early work he used schema to mean the general cognitive structures which are developing in children under the age of five.

Athey explains how children use schema to arrive at categories and classifications. For example, a baby learns by banging a wide range of objects, and by trying out a wide range of schema on a single object, whether or not the object is bangable, suckable, throwable, shakable and so on. This underlines the importance of rich and varied experience.

Over time, schema can be put together to create higher level and more powerful schemas. Schema theory can be used, for example, to explain the results obtained by Piaget in his conservation tests (see page 38). When a child is unable to say that two rows of counters are the same even though they know that there are ten in each row, Donaldson's (see page 61) explanation is that the context does not make 'human sense' to the child. Schema theory can be interpreted as suggesting that although the child has a number or quantity schema as well as a length schema they are not yet able to consider both at the same time. The dominant or more important of the two schema for young children is likely to be length and this is the concept which dominates their response to the question.

According to Athey (3) schema evolve from early action and perception. They are part of the way in which children seek to make sense of their environment and relationships.

The analysis of observations, drawings and paintings led the project team to identify a number of schemas. Children appeared to have four stages in exploring and using schema. At first, there is a period of physical action where the movement does not carry any real significance. Secondly, there is a stage when schema are used to symbolise something. Thirdly, children may begin to see the functional relationship between two things and, finally, the schema supports thought.

An example of this might be a child interested in rotation. At the first stage they might simply spend time twirling around. Over time, the twirling might be used to describe or symbolise a merry-go-round. The child may become interested in the relationship between a reel of fishing line and the way in which it acts to change the length of line – shortening and lengthening it depending on the direction in which it is turned. Finally, the child becomes able to put all these ideas into words and to reason about them.

The schema identified in the research project included:

- Vertical
- Back and forth or side to side
- Circular or rotational
- Going over, under or on top of
- Going round a boundary
- Containing and enveloping
- Going through a boundary.

For each of these Athey gives examples of the four stages.

Putting the theory into practice

Tina Bruce (4) describes the importance and usefulness of schema for identifying the consistent thread of interest that a child may have. She suggests that this can be hidden from the educator if he or she concentrates simply on the content of the child's interest. She quotes Chris Athey as saying that 'frequently ... children shift from one kind of content to another within the same period. When they do this they are accused of flitting .... and so they might be... but they are also fitting. They are fitting various kinds of content into a particular schema'.

The point about schema theory is that it is happening in practice all the time. Whatever their dominant interest of the moment children will find ways to move or represent their ideas in ways which include their preferred schema.

For staff who plan to meet children's schema, the provision must support children in a variety of ways. Children who are interested in trajectories, for example, need materials that will enable them to throw things safely and in new challenging ways.

Her influence

Schema-spotting has become an analytical tool in many early years settings. It is particularly useful with very young children whose actions can appear random. Once practitioners begin to scrutinise their observations they may see a pattern.

Comment

No work has been done on identifying the developmental aspects of schemas. It is unclear whether children get stuck on a particular preferred schema or whether they move from schema to schema. The frequency with which particular schemas were found in the movements and representations of children at different ages in the project suggests that there may be a developmental scale of schemas. This has not yet been worked on.

There is a danger that 'schema-spotting' could trivialise observations of children's learning. Simply spotting the schema may not lead to extension and support.

References
(1) Athey, C *Extending Thought in Young Children* (Paul Chapman Publishing 1990) (see page 49)
(2) Athey, C *Extending Thought in Young Children* (Paul Chapman Publishing 1990)
(3) Athey, C *Extending Thought in Young Children* (Paul Chapman Publishing 1990) (see page 78)
(4) Bruce, T *Early Childhood Education* (Hodder and Stoughton 1987) (see page 44)

Where to find out more
Early Childhood Education (2nd ed) T Bruce (Hodder and Stoughton 1997)
Drawing and Painting: Children and Visual Representation J Matthews (Paul Chapman Publishing 2003)
Thinking Children A Meade and P Cubey (New Zealand Council for Educational Research/Institute for Early Childhood Studies 1995)
Threads of Thinking C Nutbrown (Paul Chapman Publishing 1994)

His life

In 1945, after the Second World War, a group of parents in Reggio Emilia, Northern Italy, decided that they wanted to build their own school. Loris Malaguzzi, a teacher, said that the nursery was 'created and run by parents... in a devastated town, rich only in mourning and poverty', funded from 'the sale of an abandoned war tank, a few trucks, and some horses left behind by the retreating Germans' (1).

Malaguzzi was so inspired by the courage and motivation of these parents that he changed his job so that he could teach in the first centre, Villa Cella. Through his leadership and inspiration more parent-run centres grew.

In 1963, city funding was provided for a new centre and by 1967 parental pressure had led to all the parent-run schools coming under the administration of the municipality of Reggio Emilia.

The centres are characterised by the attention they give to involving everyone in learning. Parents, children, professional staff and the wider community are all seen as part of the education process. Reggio Emilia educators value all aspects of children's development. Children are viewed in terms of their strengths, not weaknesses, and are given credit for their capacity to learn. The results are seen in the aesthetic environments of the schools, the spirit of co-operation between staff, parents and children and in the quality of children's representational work.

His theory

Malaguzzi based the philosophy which he brought to the nurseries of Reggio Emilia on the work of Dewey, Piaget, Vygotsky and Erikson.

Over time, a theoretical underpinning has evolved which give the schools a distinctive style and approach. The key principles include (2):

- All children have potential;

  - Children are connected (to their family community, society, objects, symbols);
  - The reciprocity of children (meaning that they not only want to receive but to give);
  - Children are communicators;
  - The environment is the third teacher;
  - Educators are partners, nurturers and guides;
  - Educators are researchers;
  - Documentation is important for communication;
  - Parents are partners;
  - Education is about asking questions.

Putting the theory into practice

The curriculum in the Reggio Emilia pre-school centres is built around a range of visual and expressive arts. Children are given opportunities to represent their experiences, ideas, thoughts and feelings in a variety of 'languages'. Thinking and learning are believed to be promoted by the 'translation' from one language to another. So, a child may observe and draw the lions in the town square but will also be encouraged to move like a lion, paint and model lions, act out a shadow play about lions and talk about lions.

Every nursery has an atelierista whose job it is to promote children's visual, aesthetic and creative representations. The atelierista makes sure that the workshops (or ateliers), which are an integral part of provision in all the nurseries, are maintained to high standards and equipped with stimulating materials.

Malaguzzi's underlying philosophy, with its emphasis on reflection, is symbolised by the widespread use of light, glass and mirrors. Children use spotlights and overhead projectors to create images on screens and walls. Classrooms are equipped with shadow screens. Mirror lined boxes encourage children to look at reflections and mirrors are placed so that children can observe themselves and others, monitoring and rehearsing facial expressions.

Record-keeping in Reggio Emilia relies on documentation. The atelierista makes sure that documentation is kept. Children's responses to activities and experiences are recorded in photographs, videos, written observations, transcripts of children's comments and conversations, and of course children's drawings, models, paintings and other creative endeavours. Documentation is analysed and reviewed by staff in their continuous efforts to observe, identify and understand children's learning. In their view, formal assessment is only necessary if you do not believe that learning is visible.

The influence of Reggio Emilia

As the fame of the schools spread, Jerome Bruner (see pages 47-49), Lilian Katz (an internationally known American professor of early childhood education), and Howard Gardner (see pages 63-66) became interested in and excited by the work in Reggio Emilia. Howard Gardner has developed a close link with the schools, working to compare both the theory and the practice which surrounds Project Zero at Harvard University (see page 65) and the work of Reggio children.

Those who visit Reggio Emilia are impressed by the quality of the work which children produce, by the beauty of the environments created with children and by the sense of community support and involvement.

There are attempts to emulate the work of Reggio Emilia around the world, particularly in the United States. In Sweden there is a Reggio Emilia Institute. In New Zealand early years teachers receive some training in the approach.

Comment

Loris Malaguzzi's approach grew up in a particular context for a particular community. It cannot be moved from one culture to another.

A former mayor of the town said (3) that, having been subjected to a Fascist regime, the citizens had decided that 'people who conformed and obeyed were dangerous' and that it was therefore imperative 'to communicate that lesson and nurture a vision of children who can think and act for themselves'.

Peter Moss, Professor of Early Childhood Provision at London Institute of Education and a researcher at Thomas Coram Research Centre, says that

'Reggio does not offer a recipe nor a method and cannot be copied because (the) values (on which it is based) can only be lived' (4).

There are also concerns to do with race, gender and class. One parent comments that 'until recently the cultural mix wasn't an issue. It was a very wealthy area..... Now there are immigrants .... who bring problems.... The people of Reggio do not want to change' (5). Given that this is a society that has not had to deal with the challenge of cultural diversity, and where gender issues have not been high on the agenda, some writers (5) question the extent to which practitioners in this country should seek to imitate the work of Reggio Emilia.

References
(1) Malaguzzi, L 'History, ideas and basic philosophy' in Edwards, C et al (eds) *The Hundred Languages of Children – the Reggio Emilia approach to early education* (Ablex, 1993) (see page 42)
(2) Reggio's key principles have been taken from the website for the Sightlines Initiative, an organisation which seeks to build on and disseminate the practice developed in Reggio Emilia (www. sightlines-initiative.com).
(3) This comment is cited by Peter Moss on page 136 in a chapter called 'The otherness of Reggio' in *Experiencing Reggio Emilia* edited by Lesley Abbott and Cathy Nutbrown (Open University Press 2001).
(4) Moss, P 'The otherness of Reggio' in *Experiencing Reggio Emilia* edited by Lesley Abbott and Cathy Nutbrown (Open University Press, 2001)
(5) Browne, N *Gender Equity in the Early Years* (Open University Press 2004) (see page 49)

Where to find out more
The Hundred Languages of Children – the Reggio Emilia Approach to Early Education C Edwards et al (Ablex 1993)

Websites:
www.sightlines-initiative.com
http//:zerosei.comune.re.it/inter/rc_publications

The municipality has an organisation which publishes and distributes a range of books, pamphlets and videos. Full details can be found on both the Reggio Children and Sightlines-Initiative websites (see above).

Paulo Freire

PROFILE

Paolo Freire was a Brazilian social activist, educator and education theorist. During his exile he worked in many parts of the world to transform the life chances of disadvantaged groups. Once he was able to return to Brazil he set about improving the education of adults and children.

KEY DATES

1921	Born
1964	Exiled to Chile
1979	Returns to Brazil
1997	Dies

LINKS

- Fromm

His life

Paolo Freire was born in 1921 in Recife, Brazil. Freire worked with peasant workers, mainly in the impoverished areas of north-eastern Brazil, developing ways of dealing with the problems of widespread illiteracy.

Following his exile to Chile, he became engaged in educational programmes in various countries including Chile, Angola, Mozambique, Cape Verde, Guinea-Bissau and Nicaragua when he worked as a consultant for UNESCO.

Political changes in Brazil meant that Freire could return there in 1979 and following elections won by the Workers Party be became Secretary of Education. He launched several progressive programmes including those dealing with adult education, curricular restructuring, community participation and policies for democratising schools. For Freire, education was political. He emphasised the importance of praxis, which he defined as action linked to reflection.

Freire did not want his ideas to become accepted without question as he believed that education is inextricably linked to culture. Freire's theories drew on Eric Fromm's ideas (see page 18) from whom he quotes as follows (1):

'Freedom to create and to construct, to wonder and to venture, such freedom requires that the individual be active and responsible, not a slave or a well-fed cog in the machine... It is not enough that men are slaves; if social conditions further the existence of automatons, the result will not be love of life but love of death.'

His writing

Friere wrote a number of books but few have been translated into English. His most influential book was Pedagogy of the Oppressed (Penguin 1972).

His theory

Freire's work (2) was about transformation. It sought to change existing practices, rules, traditions and understandings as a way of achieving social justice and equality. He used social activism and social reconstructionism - drawing inspiration from liberation struggles in different parts of Latin America. For Freire, education should seek to make the individual a morally, intellectually and politically engaged activist so that society and its values can be transformed and so extend the possibility of justice to all.

Change theorists, such as Freire, wanted children to be able to critically analyse their daily lives.

Putting the theory into practice

Freire was concerned with changing ideas. His aim was to promote equality of opportunity by helping children to deal with the fair and unfair. He wanted them to work in an environment where they cooperated in creating a living democracy and building social action skills. The classroom for Freire, therefore, involved learners talking and exploring ideas, learning with the teacher rather than from them.

His influence

Freire worked in disadvantaged communities to increase their involvement in democracy and education. In some of those places, transformational theories have had a vital role to play in tackling inequalities and he has promoted an awareness of the power needed to transform society.

Social reconstruction requires co-operation and a genuine desire for change. For Freire, the greatest danger would be for his ideas to become tokens or slogans.

He is sometimes criticised for being too mystical. His rhetoric can be seen as simplistic, rooted in black and white. He has also been criticised as having an outmoded view of literacy and the way in which reading and writing are best acquired.

References
(1) Taken from Fromm's book *The Heart of Man*
(2) MacNaughton, G *Shaping Early Childhood* (Open University Press 2003)

Where to find out more
www.infed.org/thinkers/et-freir.htm

High/Scope

PROFILE

High/Scope is an approach that was developed by Dr David Weikart to serve children at risk of school failure in Ypsilanti, Michigan, USA. The name signifies 'high aspirations and breadth of vision'. The curriculum model is now used in more than 20 countries including UK, Ireland, Mexico, the Netherlands, Indonesia, Korea and South Africa.

KEY DATES

1962   High/Scope Perry Pre-school Project, Ypsilanti, Michigan, USA, began with the first group of 123 children
Publication of longitudinal results of the Ypsilanti Perry Pre-school Project by D Weikart et al, Monograph of the High/Scope Education Research Foundation, 1 (High/Scope Press)

1984   Publication of *Changed Lives: The Effects of the Perry Pre-school Program on Youth through Age 19* by J R Berrueta-Clement (High/Scope Press)

1990   High/Scope UK, the first Institute outside of the US, was formed

2004   Publication of *Lifetime Effects: The High/Scope Perry Pre-school Study through Age 40* by L Schweinhart (High/Scope Press)

LINKS

- Piaget
- Vygotsky
- Erikson
- Dewey

The High/Scope approach

The High/Scope approach is based on 40 years of research and practice. It centres on recognising and supporting the unique differences in children aged between two and six and developing their self-confidence by building on what they can do.

Staff encourage children to become decision-makers and problem-solvers, helping them to develop skills and traits that enable them to become successful students as they grow older. High/Scope also encourages managers to value training and encourages parents, caregivers and teachers to extend their expectations for children and themselves.

The High/Scope programme was devised by Dr David Weikart in response to the continued low achievement of students at high school in Ypsilanti, Michigan. Dr Weikart says: 'In the High/Scope approach to early childhood education, adults and children share control. We recognise that the power to learn resides in the child, hence the focus on active learning practices. When we accept that learning comes from within, we achieve a critical balance in educating young children. The adult's role is to support and guide young children through their active learning adventures and experiences.'

From 1962 to 1967, Dr Weikart and his colleagues operated the High/Scope Perry Pre-school Programme in Ypsilanti. A group of children aged three were chosen and assigned to either an intervention group or a no intervention group. The intervention group attended a high quality early years setting for two and a half hours a day for two years. The teachers also visited the children at home to work with their parents and explain the approach.

The pre-school curriculum was based on three basic criteria:

- A coherent theory about teaching and learning must guide the curriculum development process;
- Curriculum theory and practice must support each child's capacity to develop individual talents and abilities through ongoing opportunities for active learning;
- The teachers, researchers and administrators must work as partners in all aspects of the curriculum development, to ensure that theory and practice receive equal consideration.

At various intervals throughout the past 40 years researchers have gathered information on both groups from age three through to 11, and again at 14, 15, 19, 27 and 40 years old. The results have consistently shown positive outcomes, both educational and social, for the group receiving early intervention. Early results found that the programme group was less likely to need remedial support, less likely to be kept in their year group, showed greater persistence, independence, problem-solving ability and motivation.

At age 40, the latest findings show:

- Significantly more of the programme group than the no-programme group were employed (76 v 62 per cent);
- The programme group had higher earnings at both 27 and 40;
- The programme group were involved in fewer crimes;
- There was less reliance on welfare benefit and more likelihood of home ownership;
- More programme than no programme males raised their own children (57 v 30 per cent).

ASSESSMENT
- Teamwork
- Daily anecdotal notes
- Daily planning
- Child assessment

ADULT-CHILD INTERACTION
- Interaction strategies
- Encouragement
- Problem-solving approach to conflict

ACTIVE LEARNING
Initiative
Key experiences

DAILY ROUTINE
- Plan-Do-Review
- Small-group time
- Large-group time

LEARNING ENVIRONMENT
- Areas
- Materials
- Storage

Putting the theory into practice

The High/Scope approach is influenced by the writing of Jean Piaget. Piaget's theory of development supported the original curriculum team's philosophical orientation toward active learning. As the approach developed, the teachers involved in the project concentrated on the pragmatics of integrating theory and daily classroom practice.

Central principles

The wheel of learning, at the centre of which is the child – the active learner – illustrates the central principles of High/Scope (see diagram above). The sections that surround the hub will support the child to be an active learner and should be viewed as playing an equal role. These principles guide all High/Scope practitioners in their daily work.

Active learning

Through active learning - having direct and immediate experiences and deriving meaning from them through reflection - young children make sense of their world. The power of active learning comes from personal initiative. Children act on their natural desire to explore - they ask and search for answers to questions about people, materials, events and ideas that arouse their curiosity; they solve problems that stand in the way of their goals, and they generate strategies to overcome barriers.

Key experiences

The High/Scope curriculum identifies 58 developmentally appropriate Key Learning Experiences. These experiences occur naturally throughout the

time that children are in the setting each day. Staff regularly make anecdotal observations on the children's learning experiences and this forms the basis for planning and evaluating. Learning occurs in a way which meets the needs of the children and is based on their interests and prior learning.

Adult-child interaction

Active learning depends on positive adult-child interaction. Guided by an understanding of how pre-school children think and reason, adults practise positive interaction strategies - sharing control with children, focusing on children's strengths, forming authentic relationships with children, supporting play, adopting a problem-solving approach to social conflict and using encouragement rather than a system based on praise, punishment and reward. This enables children to express thoughts and feelings and confidently decide on the direction and content of the conversation, and experience partnership in dialogue.

Learning environment

The High/Scope approach places a strong emphasis on the layout of the pre-school and providing appropriate materials to enable children to make choices and decisions.

The daily routine

Adults plan a consistent routine that supports active learning. This routine enables young children to anticipate what will happen next and gives them a great deal of control over what they do during each part of their day. High/Scope provides for a balance of child and teacher initiation. The part of the daily routine which is initiated by the adult is small group time, which usually occurs after the plan-do-review cycle.

The plan-do-review process

During the plan-do-review process children learn to create and express intentions. In a group or individually, and supported by an adult, children plan what they want to do. Their planning becomes more sophisticated as they become used to the process. The youngest child may point, an older child may draw or write their plan.

Children then go on to create experiences based upon their plans. They need time for trial and error, generating new ideas, practising and succeeding. Personal independence is the key to active learning by self-motivated children. Time is given for children to act on their intentions at 'work time'.

Finally, children reflect on their experiences. A high quality curriculum must provide opportunities for children to reflect on their experiences with increasing verbal ability and logic. The time set aside for this process is called 'recall' or 'review'.

When these three components are experienced by children they develop a strong sense of self-control and self-discipline. This control is power, not over other people or things, but over oneself.

High/Scope

Understanding what is happening in the environment, realising that those around us are genuinely interested in what we say and do, and knowing that our work and effort will often lead to success, is the type of control that promotes personal satisfaction and motivates productivity.

The plan is not a straightjacket. It is seen as the beginning of a process of developing a mastery over ones own destiny.

The rest of the daily routine consists of snack time, outside time, circle time and small group time. Small group time is when the teacher plans an activity for a key experience focus. This provides the balance in the daily routine between adult and child initiated activity and all the children take part. The activity will be planned with the active learning ingredients in mind: materials, manipulation, choice, language from the child and support from the adult. Small group time is an excellent time to assess children's emerging skills and abilities.

The influence of High/Scope

The High/Scope Perry Pre-school longitudinal studies (see 'Key dates') show the long-term impact of children's involvement in the High/Scope programme.

High/Scope has also had an impact in the classroom. Positioning materials so that they are readily available to children, providing clear visual information that enables children to put resources away so that another child can easily find them and scheduling group times and opportunities for self-initiated learning are not unique to High/Scope.

They have, however, been presented in systematic ways that enable practitioners to create coherent learning environments.

High/Scope practice has been praised (1) for allowing 'children to ... see the relationships between objects and events' and for asking questions that promote problem-solving, listening and evaluation. Encouraging children to evaluate, reflect on or review what they have done is very helpful in the learning process.'

The High/Scope Educational Foundation has been active in exploring the needs of children from birth to three, infants and toddlers, and in expanding the knowledge that we have of children's development. The video, The High/Scope Approach for Under Threes, is referenced in Birth to Three Matters, the DfES framework for children birth to three. High/Scope UK has also developed courses for practitioners and parents over the past ten years.

A typical day

A typical day begins with children arriving at nursery and being greeted individually by each adult. This is the first step in a daily routine which helps children to understand and predict the order of events in their day, developing their concept of time.

Children have the opportunity to start with their own interests and ideas and are asked 'What do you plan to do today?'. They share ideas and projects with their friends and learn to negotiate, collaborate and develop independence.

Once children have planned the area or areas in which they would like to work, they go and follow their plan. They might plan to work in two or three different areas and put the product of their plans or an artefact related to their plans (such as a model, a book or a drawing/painting) in their group base on a recall table. These will be ready to discuss at recall time. Work time lasts about 45 minutes to one hour when a warning signal for tidy-up time is given by one of the children. Everybody has the responsibility of tidying up the area they have worked in and when they have finished, to go and help someone else. After tidy-up time, it is recall time. Children ask each other questions about their work:

How did you get the tube to stick?
What is that bit there?
What do you like about your model?
What did you give the baby to eat in the home corner?

Comment

There are difficulties with all approaches. Education has to be a changing process. Understanding of learning and the needs and expectations of society have changed in the past 40 years and it is important that practice develops in the light of this. When an approach is written down, there can be a tension between maintaining the approach and modifying it. If you make changes, at what point does it cease to be High/Scope? The same might be said of the Montessori approach.

The plan-do-review process could be open to criticism. Firstly, being able to articulate what you are going to do might be a problem for children for whom English is a second language (or children with language delay or learning difficulties). Many High/Scope practitioners have excellent strategies for helping children to decide, such as having pictures of resources or examples of the resources to be found in different areas. Skilled practitioners can be supportive but care must be taken that in the hands of a practitioner who does not fully understand the principles underpinning the process that it is not reduced to a child simply choosing a picture of a pair of scissors and then being told that they planned to be in the workshop so they need to stay there.

Reference
(1) MacNaughton, G Shaping Early Childhood (Open University Press 2003) (The quote is cited by MacNaughton on page 361 and is taken from Spodek and Saracho, 1994)

Where to find out more
Educating Young Children Hohmann, M and Weikart, D P (High/Scope Press 1995)

Finding the Balance: The contribution of High/Scope to developing quality relationships in two NCH projects by J Santer et al (NCH, 2001)

Useful address:
High/Scope UK provides advice and support and a range of resources for practitioners using the approach.

High/Scope UK
High/Scope Institute
192 Maple Road
London SE20 8HT
Tel: 020 8676 0220
Email: highscope@btconnect.com
www.high-scope.org.uk

Margaret Donaldson

Her life

Margaret Donaldson is Emeritus Professor of Developmental Psychology at the University of Edinburgh, where she has studied and worked throughout her career. She was born in Paisley in 1926, the eldest of three children.

When Donaldson began her career in developmental psychology, behaviourism was the dominant theory. She spent a term with Piaget in 1957. Martin Hughes (1) writes that 'she came back impressed by his methods and the scale of his theorising, but not convinced he was necessarily right'.

She was also influenced by Vygotsky, and by Bruner, with whom she worked at Harvard during the 1960s.

In the same decade, Donaldson set up a nursery in the Department of Psychology at the University of Edinburgh. Her observations of three- to five-year-old children there led to the insights that formed the basis of her book, Children's Minds.

Her writing

▓ Children's Minds (Fontana 1978)
▓ Early Childhood Development and Education: Readings in Psychology with R Grieve and C Pratt (Blackwell 1983)
▓ Human Minds (Penguin 1992)

Her theory

Donaldson came to the conclusion that children's errors or misunderstandings came about because they were not simply responding to what they were being asked to do but were also seeking to understand the meaning of the task or request. They were seeking to make 'human sense' of the situation.

The notion of embedded and disembedded thinking is central to Donaldson's theory. Thinking which is embedded or situated in a familiar context makes human sense and so is more easily understood by children and open to reason. When children are asked to think outside the limits of human sense, in unfamiliar, unrealistic or abstract contexts, their thinking is disembedded and fails to make sense to them.

Donaldson has applied these ideas to Piaget's work. She shows how young children's apparent limitations, which Piaget attributed to their stage of development, are often a result of the task failing to make human sense to them. In Children's Minds, Donaldson describes her own experimental work and that of her students.

She first tries to build on and modify Piaget's theory of egocentrism. The three mountains test, which Piaget devised to explore young children's ability to take another point of view, does not allow children to demonstrate their understanding, accordiing to Donaldson. She says that Piaget's task is disembedded and so presents particular difficulties. When Martin Hughes wished to explore children's ability to take another's point of view he devised an embedded test in which a policeman and a naughty boy were placed on a board with intersecting walls. Children were asked to place the boy where he could not be seen by the policeman. Because this task was embedded in a context which children could understand, a

far higher proportion of them were able to demonstrate an ability to think in a non-egocentric way than in Piaget's experiments.

Secondly, she describes experiments by James McGarrigle which set out to refine some of Piaget's conservation tasks. In one of the classic Piagetian tasks children are shown two rows of ten counters, and asked whether the two lines are the same or different. When the children have agreed that they are the same, one line is extended so that it looks longer than the other – even though it has the same number of counters. Young children tend to say that the longer line has more counters – although they often know that each line still contains ten objects. McGarrigle devised some variations on this test which involved a teddy bear. This gave a context for the questions and children were far more likely to respond correctly.

Donaldson argues in Children's Minds that 'The better you are at tackling problems without having to be sustained by human sense, the more likely you are to succeed in our education system' (2).

Her theories are often focused on educational failure. This is reflected in her view that 'the hope then is that reading can be taught in such a way as greatly to enhance the child's reflective awareness not only of language as a symbolic system, but of the processes of his own mind' (3).

She stresses that feeling and thought are given the same value – one is not more important than the other. The stages or modes are point mode, line mode, construct mode and transcendent mode (see left).

Putting the theory into practice

Margaret Donaldson's work led many practitioners (and researchers) to reassess the idea of readiness to learn and psychological testing methods. This in turn has meant that those working with young children are less ready to accept test findings in which children are required to think in disembedded or formal ways.

Piagetian theory led many practitioners, particularly during the 1960s, to think of children having a ceiling on their thinking. Donaldson's challenges to those theories encouraged practitioners to seek out what children are able to do rather than emphasising what they cannot do. This does not mean that Donaldson rejected child-centred education. Indeed, she suggests that the education of young children should be based on a decentred approach. She deliberately chose this Piagetian term because she believed that in order to educate young children effectively, practitioners must 'decentre' and try to present things from the child's viewpoint.

Her influence

In the introduction to Early Childhood Development and Education Donaldson identifies three trends in developmental psychology. She

Mode of thinking	Indicative age/ may be apparent from:	Description
Point mode	2-3 months	Thinking is concerned with the here and now
Line mode	8-9 months	Thinking includes specific events recalled from specific events
Construct mode	3-4 years	Thinking involves considering how things are in the world or the general nature of things. There are two forms: the intellectual construct mode (such as doing sums); and the value-sensing construct mode (such as appreciating a painting or a piece of music).
Transcendent	not achieved by all	Thinking moves beyond mode time and space. There are two forms: the intellectual transcendent mode (such as logic); and the value-sensing transcendent mode (such as spiritual or religious thought).

Margaret Donaldson

suggests that we are now able to see more clearly the importance of interpersonal relationships in developing language and thought. Secondly, we have begun to understand the special demands that are made on children when we ask them to undertake disembedded tasks. Thirdly, we are much more aware of the importance in attempting to understand children's learning of focusing on what they can do rather than what they cannot do.

Donaldson has challenged the orthodoxy of both teaching and developmental psychology and identified the importance (and some of the limitations) of child-centred education. She is not alone in stressing the equal value of intellect and emotion – but her clear and accessible writing have made this apparent to a wide audience.

Comment

Although Donaldson refers to educational applications of her work, they are not well developed. Practical ideas may have made it possible for practitioners to engage more with the problems presented by Piagetian theory and prevented some of the backlash against child-centred approaches.

References

(1) Hughes, M (Routledge 2001) 'Margaret Donaldson' in Palmer, J A (ed) *Fifty Modern Thinkers on Education* (see page 176)
(2) Donaldson, M *Children's Minds* (Fontana 1978) (see page 77)
(3) Donaldson, M *Children's Minds* (Fontana 1978) (see page 99)

More information

Children's Minds Margaret Donaldson (Fontana 1978)

'Margaret Donaldson' in *Fifty Modern Thinkers on Education* by J A Palmer (Routledge 2001) (pages 175 - 181)

Howard Gardner

His life

Howard Gardner is Professor of Cognition and Education at Harvard University but has worked in many areas of psychology. He has been strongly influenced by Bruner (see pages 47-49) with whom he worked early in his career. Gardner is best known for his book, Frames of Mind, in which he sets out his multiple intelligence theory (MIT).

He admits that he has been influenced by the death of his elder brother, aged only eight, before Howard was even born (1). He did not know about this tragedy until he discovered a newspaper cutting reporting it. He claims that his motivation for success as a pianist and scholar came from his sense of having to make up in some way for the death of his brother.

In his academic career he was highly influenced by Erik Erikson, one of his tutors at Harvard, and from whom he learned to value careful observation, to regard human personality as the central concern of psychology and to focus on developmental psychology. His early career was unorthodox and his influences unusually diverse.

Firstly, he won a scholarship and spent a year in London, reading and visiting theatres and galleries. Secondly, he got a job with Bruner who was developing his curriculum project 'Man: a course of study'. Through this project he was introduced to the work of Piaget and Levi-Strauss who studied diverse cultural practices. He took a job for a short time as a teacher of young children and spent some time working with schizophrenic patients.

His writing

Gardner has written many books, dating back to the early 1970s. As well as Frames of Mind (Fontana), titles of particular interest to early childhood practitioners include:

- The Arts and Human Development (1973)
- Artful Scribbles (1980)
- The Unschooled Mind: how children think and how schools should teach (1993)

His theory

Gardner regards intelligence as being 'too important to be left to intelligence testers' (2). He suggests that 'we must figure out how intelligence and morality can work together to create a world in which a great variety of people will want to live'.

Multiple intelligence theory arose out of Gardner's dissatisfaction with the dominant views of intelligence and learning early in his career. In his book, Frames of Mind, Gardner sets out the contributions of major theorists to our thinking about intelligence. He cites Charles Darwin, the evolutionist, as doing 'more than any other figure to stimulate scientific study of the mind' (3).

He underlines the role of Gesell, who focused on the genetic factors that shape learning. Gesell's research with twins suggested that many aspects of children's maturation were determined by their biology. He set out what Gardner calls 'the orderly milestones of development' (4) by setting up experiments where one twin would be given special training in, for example, climbing stairs while the other was not given any support. In many cases, training made no difference to the twins' ability to perform physical tasks (6).

Gardner compares this view to that of the behaviourist, Skinner. Skinner believed that 'a human being could learn to do almost anything that his surroundings dictated' (5). Nurture, or systematic training, could enable rats to run mazes and pigeons to play table tennis.

PROFILE

Howard Gardner has worked in many fields of psychology. A self-styled 'old student of the brain', he developed the multiple intelligence theory. Gardner's work continues to influence current understanding of learning and creativity.

KEY DATES

1943	Born in Pennsylvania, USA
1961	Begins studying at Harvard University, where he has remained throughout his career.
1983	*Frames of Mind* is published, setting out multiple intelligence theory

LINKS

- Erikson (psychoanalytical theorist)
- Piaget
- Bruner

Howard Gardner

Gardner also discusses the contribution of Piaget, whom he describes as 'beyond question the single dominant thinker in his field' (6). However, he thought that Piaget placed too little emphasis on the importance of the emotions and of motivation in learning and too much emphasis on logic and number. Gardner also criticises Piaget's notion of staged development with the implications that:

- The stage of development in one area of development is tied to the stage of development in another area.
- As the learner moves from one stage of development to another, they leave behind earlier aspects of development. Gardner, like Bruner, says that earlier ways of thinking and exploring (such as play) are not left behind as we move towards abstract thinking but can be drawn on to support learning in new areas or experiences.

Gardner's work on multiple intelligences arose from his dissatisfaction with the notion of intelligence as something that could be seen or measured and represented as an IQ score. He has set out to explore 'how people are intelligent rather than how much intelligence they have' (7). He defines intelligence as 'the ability to solve problems or to create products that are valued within one or more cultural settings' (8). He regards the emergence of intelligences as dependent on the opportunities offered to children within a particular context or culture.

Gardner suggests that specific intelligences can be identified because:

- damage to specific areas of the brain causes specific kinds of impairment such as with language;
- savants and prodigies show specific gifts in particular areas such as mathematics and music;
- it is possible to test specific areas, such as spatial awareness, in different ways and to find correlations between these tests;
- a defined developmental process has been identified - again this is the case with language;
- the behaviour can be encoded in a symbol system. Language and mathematics can be written as well as spoken and read.

Linguistic intelligence
Linguistic intelligence is being demonstrated when we use language to:
- convince others
- remember
- explain events, ideas and feelings - this includes story, poetry and metaphors when we say, for example, the sky was a billowing tent
- reflect on language itself, what is called metalinguistic analysis.

Logical-mathematical intelligence
This intelligence:
- has particular importance in the West
- is helpful in dealing with some kinds of problems
- should not be seen as more important than others

Bodily-kinaesthetic intelligence
This intelligence is concerned with all the ways in which humans express ideas in physical ways. Gardner suggests that bodily-kinaesthetic intelligence is:
- concerned with the relationship between the mental and physical, the reflective and the active;
- shaped by cultural expectations.
Gardner (9) reminds us of work in Reggio Emilia when he writes: 'There are languages other than words, languages of symbols and languages of nature. There are languages of the body.' These might include dance, gesture, facial expressions and so on.

Musical intelligence
Gardner suggests that this intelligence:
- is the earliest to emerge
- captures the spirit of emotions
- has links to our evolution
- there are many with unusual talent
- like other intelligences, it does not stand alone. A musician needs more than musical intelligence - he or she may need spatial intelligence and bodily kinaesthetic intelligence and particularly interpersonal intelligence.

Spatial intelligence
Spatial intelligence:
- often cannot be expressed through other intelligences. While, for example, children can both draw (bodily-kinaesthetic intelligence) and talk (linguistic intelligence) about an event, thinking about space may not be so readily represented in other ways;
- is concerned with the recognition and manipulation of wide space as well as more confined areas (such as jigsaw puzzles).

Naturalist intelligence
Gardner suggests that 'the popularity of dinosaurs among five-year-olds is no accident!' because it is an indication of our evolutionary, naturalist intelligence (10). He goes on to identify aspects of naturalist intelligence as being seen in:
- our ability to recognise members of a group
- our phenomenal ability to identify and recognise patterns
- our propensity to categorise and classify animals, birds, insects, plants etc.

In the first edition of Frames of Mind, published in 1983, Gardner listed seven intelligences which he had identified by using the criteria above. At that stage he suggested that the intelligences were:

- linguistic intelligence
- musical intelligence
- logical-mathematical intelligence
- spatial intelligence
- bodily-kinaesthetic intelligence
- interpersonal (interactions with others) and
- intrapersonal (understanding of self) intelligences.

Later, he added naturalist intelligence (concerned with nature, seasons, plant categorisation) and suggested that the two personal intelligences should be seen as permeating all others. He considered and rejected the idea of spiritual intelligence but proposed that we all have an existential intelligence (awareness of something beyond us and our lives) but this intelligence has not been defined in the same detail as others.

Gardner considers that these intelligences are present in each of us depending on the extent to which our background, experiences and opportunities have allowed us to develop them. He writes (11):

> 'Every time we are exposed to a new individual - in person or in spirit - our own horizons broaden.... Because our genes and our experiences are unique and because our brains must figure out meanings, no two selves, no two consciousnesses, no two minds are exactly alike. Each of us is therefore situated to make a unique contribution to the world.'

For Gardner, creativity is not the same as intelligence. He believes that people tend to be creative only in one or two domains or areas, rather than generally creative. He writes of Big-C creativity and assumes that this is the quality found in people like Mozart, Gandhi and Marie Curie. For him, the 'acid test' of creativity is, quite simply, has this person's work changed the nature of the subject itself?

Putting the theory into practice

There have been a number of attempts to put multiple intelligence theory into practice, particularly in Australia and the United States. At Harvard University, where Gardner works, there is a long-term project called Project Zero or Project Spectrum in which a number of academics have sought to put their theories into practice. The project is based on the assumption that 'each child exhibits a distinctive profile of different abilities, or multiple intelligences' but that 'rather than being fixed, these intelligences can be enhanced by an educational environment rich in stimulating materials and activities' (12). You can read more about this research project in a series of books edited by Gardner, Feldman and Krechevsky (see below).

In this country, Alistair Smith has developed an approach for schools with pupils of all ages called Accelerated Learning which emphasises multiple intelligences and looks at ways, for example, of supporting bodily-

Howard Gardner

kinaesthetic or spatial intelligences rather than relying on the narrowly emphasised linguistic and logical-mathematical aspects of learning.

Gardner admires the work that is done in Reggio Emilia. He regards as important their philosophy of promoting:

- co-operative learning;
- artistic work;
- the involvement of parents and community; and
- discovery and debate.

In a comparison of Project Zero and Reggio Emilia (13) he makes the following points:

- While Project Zero began with theories, Reggio Emilia began with 'promising practices' that were developed within a theoretical superstructure.
- The emphasis in Reggio Emilia is on visual and graphic modes of representation while in Project Zero the focus is on linguistic and musical intelligences.

His influence

Multiple intelligence theory has captured popular imagination and a lot of interest is shown in finding ways to put it into practice.

Gardner has prompted popular work by other academics, such as Daniel Goleman (see pages 79-80), whose best-selling books on emotional literacy may owe much to Gardner.

Comment

There is a danger in the application of multiple intelligence theory that practitioners will trivialise. Gardner claims that some schools are asking pupils whether they have exercised their intelligences today.

The roots of intelligences are not always clear. For example, it is difficult to think about how personal intelligences might be subjected to a symbol system.

The intelligences do not lend themselves to assessment nor are they open to testing. Gardner's selection of intelligences has also been criticised (and changed over time). In answer to this, Gardner claims that he is less concerned with which intelligences exist than the fact that everyone has a unique mix of strengths and weaknesses.

References
(1) Gardner, H *To Open Minds* (Basic Books Inc 1989)
(2) Gardner, H *Intelligence Reframed* (Basic Books Inc 1999) (see page 3)
(3) Gardner, H *Frames of Mind* (2nd ed) (Fontana 1993) (see page 24)
(4) Gardner, H *Frames of Mind* (2nd ed) (Fontana 1993) (see page 24)
(5) Gardner, H *Frames of Mind* (2nd ed) (Fontana 1993) (see page 25)
(6) Gardner, H *Frames of Mind* (2nd ed) (Fontana, 1993) (see page 28)
(7) Krechevsky, M and Seidel, S 'Minds at work: applying multiple intelligences in the classroom' in Collins, J and Cook, D (eds) *Understanding Learning: Influences and Outcomes* (Paul Chapman Publishing in association with The Open University 2001) (see page 49)
(8) See Gardner (1999) on page 33
(9) Gardner (1993) cites Mailer on page 208
(10) See Gardner (1999) on page 50
(11) See Gardner (1999) on pages 218-9
(12) Chen at al *Building on Children's Strengths: the experience of Project Spectrum* (Teachers' College Press 1998) (page xiii)
(13) Guidici, C et al (2001) *Making learning Visible Reggio: Project Zero and Reggio Children* (page 338)

Where to find out more
Accelerated Learning A Smith (Network Educational Press 1996)

'Minds at work: applying multiple intelligences in the classroom' by M Krechevsky and S Seidel in *Understanding Learning: influences and outcomes* J Collins and D Cook (eds) (Paul Chapman Publishing/The Open University 2001)

Te Whariki

PROFILE

Te Whariki is the New Zealand early years curriculum. It uses learning stories as an approach to assessment and places the learner at the heart of the assessment process. It was published in 1996.

Background

Throughout the 1980s early childhood specialists and practitioners in New Zealand worked with each other and with government to develop a unified approach to early childhood care and education. In a country with two dominant cultures (Maori and Western), they were concerned to produce curriculum guidelines that could be agreed and shared by all. Te Whariki (the New Zealand early years curriculum) was the result of their collaboration.

Te Whariki is rooted in an assumption that all children are 'competent and confident learners and communicators, healthy in mind, body and spirit, secure in their sense of belonging and in the knowledge that they make a valued contribution to society'. They are seen as having an abundance of skills, abilities or competencies (1). Whariki is a Maori word which means 'woven mat'. The curriculum is seen as being woven from principles, aims and goals and appropriate practice - all of which are described in detail in the document.

New Zealand has had a diverse pattern of provision for early childhood care and education. Te Whariki recognises this diversity and offers the guidance as a framework. It suggests that diversity occurs in early childhood settings because of:

- Different cultural perspectives - not just the Maori and English-speaking communities but a number of Pacific Islands that have their own language and culture.
- Differences in the pattern of attendance - full- or part-time, daily or just one or two days a week.
- Organisational, philosophical and environmental differences - Is the provision based in a home? Is the philosophical underpinning based on Montessori or Steiner? Is it described as a kindergarten, a playgroup, day nursery?
- Different local resources and levels of community involvement depending on whether the setting is in an urban or rural community; whether parents are working or not.
- Differences in the emphasis in each setting - perhaps a member of staff is particularly interested in music, or the focus is on story;
- The age range.

Content

The principles are interwoven with five strands. These are:

- well-being;
- belonging;
- contribution;
- communication; and
- exploration.

Each strand is described as an aim and has three or four goals. For each goal there are learning outcomes – more than 100 across the five aims. There is also guidance on management and organisation of the environment for each goal, together with examples of what adults must do to support children in achieving the relevant outcomes. Examples relevant for babies, toddlers and young children are given for each goal.

The curriculum document states that it 'is founded on the following aspirations for children:

- to grow up as competent and confident learners and communicators;
- healthy in mind, body and spirit;
- secure in their sense of belonging; and
- in the knowledge that they make a valued contribution to society'.

It also says that provision must be based on key experiences that are appropriate to children in the following ways:

- humanly;
- nationally;
- culturally;
- developmentally;
- individually; and
- educationally.

The underlying principles of:

- empowerment,
- holistic development,
- family and community, and
- relationships
- are to be used to inform assessments of children.

The curriculum framework was developed with the support of all sectors of early childhood care and education.

Putting the theory into practice

The content of the curriculum is not based on traditional subject areas. It has been suggested (2) that Te Whariki is concerned with children as they are now. It is not aimed at preparing them for the next stage of schooling. The intention is that teaching and learning should be based entirely on children's interests.

The factors associated with the successful use of Te Whariki in early childhood settings are:

- an environment which is 'print-saturated'
- staff that are responsive, involved in children's play and who ask open-ended questions.

The influence of Te Whariki

A distinctive approach to assessment has evolved in conjunction with Te Whariki. Learning stories (3), as the assessment or observations are called, keep track of children's strengths and interests in relation to the five strands of the curriculum. Just as practitioners in Reggio Emilia believe that the learning process can be observed and recorded in their documentation so those following Te Whariki regard the strands of learning as being observable.

The table below shows the aspect that is believed to be both characteristic of and observable within each strand. Notes on each of these are recorded and together create what is called a learning story. The table also shows 'children's voice' questions which have been identified as aspects of practice which can be used to evaluate the quality of provision.

Learning stories have many advantages over other forms of assessment because they (5):

- Involve children's relationships and interactions with others, which means that learning is observed within a context and not as a set of isolated skills.
- Focus on what matters to the child, rather than on the demands and expectations of others.
- Are collected in natural, rather than contrived, situations.
- Pay attention to the context and the people involved in the observation.
- Enable practitioners to begin with children's strengths and help them to pinpoint difficulties.

Strand of Te Whariki	Related dispositions	Observable aspect	Child's voice questions (4)	
Belonging	Courage and curiosity	Taking an interest	Do you appreciate and understand my interests and abilities and those of my family?	Do you know me?
Well-being	Trust and playfulness	Being involved	Do you meet my daily needs with care and sensitive consideration?	Can I trust you?
Exploration	Perseverance	Persisting with difficulty, challenge & uncertainty	Do you engage my mind, offer challenges and extend my world?	Do you let me fly?
Communication	Confidence	Expressing a point of view or feeling	Do you invite me to communicate and respond to my own particular efforts?	Do you hear me?
Contribution	Responsibility	Taking responsibility	Do you encourage and facilitate my endeavours to be part of the wider group?	Is this place fair for us?

Comment

Te Whariki is widely seen as a successful approach which shows respect for children and their learning and which has sought to identify and value diversity. However, two areas of criticism have emerged, both to do with inclusive practice.

Throughout the Te Whariki document there is an emphasis on inclusion. Joy Cullen, a Professor of Early Education from New Zealand, has suggested (6) that despite this, many children with special educational needs in New Zealand early years settings are marginalised because they are 'Velcroed' to their support worker, and/ or because they do not have strategies or opportunities to become involved with other children in their play.

Although the curriculum was designed to be bicultural, MacNaughton (2003) suggests that the needs and interests of some minority groups may not be represented in its approach and that it may not be possible to produce the 'one size fits all' standards which New Zealand practitioners worked hard to create.

References
(1) Thorp, M Keynote lecture 'Key times for play' at London Metropolitan University, 2003 (Maggie Thorp used this term at a lecture she gave to launch the book she co-wrote with Julia Manning-Morton called *Key Times for Play*)

(2) Fleer et al 'A Framework for conceptualising early childhood education' in Anning, A, Cullen, J and Fleer, M (eds) *Early Childhood Education: society and culture* (Sage Publications 2004)
(3) Carr, M *Assessing Children's Learning in Early Childhood Settings* (New Zealand Council for Educational Research 1998)
(4) Podmore, V 'Questioning Evaluation Quality in Early Childhood' in Anning, A, Cullen, J and Fleer, M (eds) *Early Childhood Education: society and culture* (Sage Publications 2004) (see page 153)
(5) Cullen, J 'Adults co-constructing professional knowledge' in Anning, A, Cullen, J and Fleer, M (eds) *Early Childhood Education: society and culture* (Sage Publications 2004) (see page 73)
(6) Cullen, 2004

Where to find out more
Te Whariki: Developmentally Appropriate Programmes in Early Childhood Services New Zealand Ministry of Education (Learning Media 1996)
Quality in Diversity on Early Learning Early Childhood Education Forum (NCB 1998)
Assessing Children's Learning in Early Childhood Settings M Carr (New Zealand Council for Educational Research 1988)

Websites:
www.minedu.govt.nz
www.tki.org.nz

Forest schools

Forest schools are an integral part of early childhood education in Denmark. England's first forest school for nursery children opened in Bridgwater, Somerset in 1995 and provision is growing throughout Britain. There are now about 150 forest school programmes or groups in England, 27 in Wales and ten in Scotland.

Background

Forest schools are a unique way of building independence and self-esteem in young children.

They originated in Sweden in the 1950s as a way of teaching children about the natural world. The idea was adopted by Denmark where they have become an important part of early years provision.

In 1995, a team from Bridgwater College, Somerset, went to Denmark on an exchange visit. They observed children from five to seven years of age being taken to local woodland and allowed to explore the outdoor environment. They were so impressed that, on their return, they set up a forest school – the first of its kind in the UK - at the Children's Centre, Bridgwater College. This has now become a valuable model for others and the college provides training for forest school leaders and staff.

The forest school philosophy has captured the imagination of many early years professionals. In 2002, a seminar was held at Bishops Wood Centre in Worcester to assess the national interest. As a result, a Forest School England network was created with support from the Forest Education Initiative (FEI). This is now a constituted group. FEI has drafted a list of criteria that ensures safe practice in forest schools. It has also played a lead role in developing forest schools in Wales.

Putting the theory into practice

The very first forest school in Bridgwater was set up in a basic and different way to the Denmark culture - small groups of six to eight children were taken onto the college sports field next to the children's centre. Gradually, the time outdoors was extended and children clearly enjoyed the freedom of being outside.

After the first successful year, plans were made to expand and develop the provision. A woodland area and a minibus were leased. The children were taken regularly to forest school sessions, accompanied by nursery nurse students, a key worker, forest school leader and a member of the children's centre management team.

Each year the opportunities for the children, staff and students changed and improved. Now all the children aged three and over who attend the children's centre are given the chance to take part. All the students who will join in forest school sessions go on a compulsory three-day residential to prepare them. Before the first outing a parents' evening is held to emphasise the benefits and for parents to voice concerns.

Some children are given priority of attendance - these include children with challenging behaviour or identified as having additional or specific needs. From taking part in forest school, children such as these have been observed to develop control over their behaviour, improved concentration and independence and develop their social and emotional skills. Other children previously timid and lacking in confidence within the normal nursery environment have become confident in their own abilities within the forest and are seen to move away from reliance on adults.

The children quickly learn the boundaries within which they must work. They respond to the sense of freedom and stick to the few rules laid down for their safety. They go out in all weathers, all year round, exploring and learning from the seasons and environment changes. Suitable clothing can be provided so that children get the most out of messy opportunities.

The woodland is secure - it is in the middle of fields and entirely fenced. Because of this security, it is possible to encourage children to move away from adult interaction and become more responsible for each other and for themselves. A central camp fire and semi-permanent shelter for wood storage have been built in the woods. An old lock-up cabin acts as a secure storage unit for the tools and equipment.

At Bridgwater College Children's Centre, the curriculum of individual forest school sessions varies considerably for a number of reasons, including weather conditions, levels of staffing, group dynamics, and children's moods and interest.

However, all children follow a curriculum which enables them to make as much progress as possible towards the Early Learning Goals. Every single one of the goals is worked towards throughout the year of the child attending forest school. The child's knowledge and understanding of the

world, language, mathematics, creative, physical, personal and social development underpin the whole forest school philosophy.

Children are taught how to use full-size adult tools such as saws, tenon saws and pen-knives safely. They are shown how to light and deal with fires in a controlled supervised environment. By using adult equipment, showing and preparing children, they will act in a mature and sensible way.

All children's centre staff have undergone some forest school training. Some may take a specific Forest School Leaders Award. In the past, children used to be able to experience a sense of freedom which then influenced their lifelong learning. At forest schools children are able to experience that now.

Theories about outdoor play

Friedrich Froebel talked of kindergartens – gardens of children or for children – and saw the garden as the best environment for young children's learning and development. Before then, Jean-Jacques Rousseau and Heinrich Pestalozzi, both important influences on Froebel's work, had emphasised the importance of children's interaction with nature. Robert Owen believed that children should spend substantial amounts of time each day outdoors.

By the beginning of the twentieth century, Margaret McMillan was trying to promote children's health, at first by establishing a night camp, where children at risk of contracting tuberculosis could sleep

Forest Schools

outdoors. The nursery school she opened in Deptford had a large garden and children were encouraged to play and rest outdoors. She later set up a large, outdoor residential camp in Wrotham, Kent so that children from Deptford could experience the countryside.

In 1916, the Order of Woodcraft Chivalry was established as an 'amalgam of religion, ritual, tradition, discipline and mystical expression, all coming together in a radical movement opposed to the given social structure' (1). Children from four to eight years of age were known as elves.

Susan Isaacs encouraged children to make good use of outdoor space in developing exploration and enquiry. In the period between the two world wars many experimental and progressive schools and movements developed. Amongst them was the Forest School that opened in the New Forest, Hampshire, in 1928, inspired by the work of the Order of Woodcraft Chivalry. It was co-educational, governed by a council of children, with gentle discipline and an informal curriculum. It emphasised the role of arts and crafts in learning.

In 1929, Chelsea Open-Air Nursery School was established. The American benefactor who established the school claimed that she was building it for 'the cripples of Chelsea', children who were so over-privileged as to be disadvantaged by not being allowed to face physical challenges and take risks.

Outdoor play remains an important part of early childhood provision in the UK.

Comment

Reference
(1) Selleck, R J W *English Primary Education and the Progressives 1914 – 1939* (Routledge and Kegan Paul 1972) (see pge 38)

Where to find out more
Forest Education Initiative (FEI) aims to increase the understanding and appreciation, particularly among young people, of the environmental, social, and economic potential of trees, woodlands and forests. The UK is split into four regions (England, Scotland, North Wales and South Wales), each with their own co-ordinator. Check their website to find the coordinator for your area: www.foresteducation.org.uk

For general information on outdoor provision:
Exercising Muscles and Minds by Marjorie Ouvry (National Children's Bureau 2003)

Outdoor Play in the Early Years by Helen Bilton (David Fulton 1998)

Learning through Landscapes is a charitable organisation that campaigns for children's right to decent school grounds and provides support and advice on developing the learning potential of outdoor spaces. Learning through Landscapes, 3rd Floor, Southside Offices, The Law Courts, Winchester SO23 9DL. Tel: 01962 846258. www.ltl.org.uk

www.teachernet.gov.uk/growingschools

Most practitioners know that children learn through play, but still sometimes undervalue play. Many do not understand how to support its development effectively and extend children's learning. Some are anxious about the lack of control they may have in play situations and are uncertain about how to manage a playful environment. Others do not feel able to articulate the arguments which support play as a means of learning or do not feel confident about planning for play in ways which meet the demands of heads and Ofsted inspectors.

Research for the DfES, led by Janet Moyles (1), found that few early years practitioners could explain why play is an important vehicle for learning.

What is play?

A simple definition of play is hard to come by. Tina Bruce (2) sees play as part of a network of development and learning which also includes first-hand experience, games with rules and representations, including painting, dancing, dramatic and imaginative play. Bruce suggests that play co-ordinates learning. The Curriculum Guidance for the Foundation Stage says that: 'Children do not make a distinction between 'play' and 'work' and neither should practitioners.'

Jennie Lindon (3) defines play as 'a range of activities, undertaken for their own interest, enjoyment or the satisfaction that results'. This is a useful working definition. Children must feel motivated and in control of their play. If an adult starts to take over, it stops feeling like play to children.

Play must be open-ended. There should be no required outcome for everyone to achieve. Instead, each child should be able to explore in their own way, and come to their own conclusions or achieve their own goals.

In play, children draw on and develop their past experiences and are prompted by their interaction with materials and other people to explore new knowledge, language and skills. Children's play always has a purpose for the child. The child who seems to be aimlessly pouring water may be practising a newly gained skill, may be reliving the experience of seeing a waterfall or may be feeling anxious or sad and gaining comfort from this calming activity. However, the purpose may not be apparent to adults.

It is this lack of certainty about play, and that it cannot be controlled, which worries many parents and practitioners. The learning that takes place during or as a result of play can often not be seen. Parents may put pressure on practitioners to get their children to produce work on paper because they think that this is evidence of learning. A knowledgeable practitioner is able to expose the limitations of paper-based exercises for young children. By sharing their observations of children's play and explaining to parents what they show about children's thinking and learning, parents can be led to a better understanding of the value of play. For example, children show much more sophisticated levels of understanding of number and quantity in role play when calculating what is needed for a picnic than they do when poring over a worksheet. In play, children see the point of what they are doing and thinking about, stretching themselves to the limit of their abilities. This is often not the case when they are asked to complete an adult-directed task.

Why is play important for early learning?

All of us learn best when we want to do something and are least likely to learn when we are being made to do something that doesn't interest us. Children are naturally drawn to play experiences and concentrate for long periods in their self-chosen play.

PROFILE

You may believe in the value of teaching through play but do you find it easy to say why or put it into practice? It is important to be able to explain the theory behind what you do. It is helpful if you are challenged by parents, but also because it helps you to have a better understanding of how best to support children's learning and development.

This section includes material written by Margaret Edgington first published in Practical Pre-School magazine (Issue 36) as an article called 'The value of play'.

Learning through play

Play offers children the chance to be in control, and to feel competent, within relevant, meaningful and open-ended experiences, for example reading and writing with a real purpose and without fear of getting it wrong (such as spontaneously taking a message when on the telephone in role play or taking on a powerful role such as the mum or the doctor).

In their play children are able to meet their own needs and to make sense of their own often confusing world. Play involves exploring feelings, ideas, materials, relationships and roles, making connections between one experience and another and representing ideas, objects and environments. Opportunities within play to use one thing to represent another (for example a block as a mobile phone) lay important foundations for the later use of abstract symbols, such as letters and numbers, to represent ideas.

As they get older, children begin to develop longer more complex story lines in their play. This is a vital foundation for writing.

Play encourages creativity and imagination. It is intellectually, socially, emotionally, physically and linguistically challenging and encourages children to work in depth (alone and with others). It can offer all children the chance to explore and learn at their own pace and stage of development. It has a crucial role in enabling children to consolidate learning, particularly at a time when the pace is too fast for some children.

Play is important because it enables adults to observe children at their highest level of competence and to see their ideas, concerns and interests. Lev Vygotsky (see pages 39-41) said that in their play, children are 'a head taller than themselves'. Early years practitioners who take time to observe their children at play will know exactly what he meant.

Theories about play

Play has been linked to a number of different theories about young children's learning and development (4). The different views or arguments for play are described as:

- The romantic argument – the child is considered as a whole; play is part of children's nature and children are happy when playing and learning. This view is linked to Froebel's theory.
- The behaviourist argument – linked to Skinner's theory. It suggests that after learning children deserve to play. Play is used as a reward.
- The therapeutic argument – as in the psychoanalytical theories of Freud and others, children are seen as struggling with fears. Play helps children to deal with fears and anxieties but it can also help them to learn to empathise with others. This can help children to develop awareness of how others feel and how to manage their own emotions.

- The cognitive argument - more recent theories of play emphasise its contribution to the development of problem-solving, creativity, communication and developing understanding of social rules. These ideas are most firmly linked to Piaget and Vygotsky. However, neuroscience and current developmental psychology is underlining this argument.
- The economic argument – Marie Guha (a former teacher trainer who worked at Goldsmith's College, London) proposes that if practitioners take all these arguments into account then it makes economic sense to support play – learning will be more effective if we use effective and relevant approaches which include play.
- The biological argument – scientists and psychologists are coming to the view that since playfulness is present in all humans it must have a biological function. It has been suggested that play supports the development of creativity and imagination which is essential to the development of the flexible and adaptable human brain.

Making time for play

Children today are growing up in a society where they have:

- much less freedom to play out of doors;
- less opportunity to socialise and play with other children away from an adult;
- less opportunity for play in mixed age groups - not only is there less street play but most children come from smaller families;
- more visual input from television, computers, videos and pictures in books, together with fewer opportunities to listen and create mental images.

When adults argue that 'we didn't play when we were at school and it didn't do us any harm' they are forgetting that they had rich opportunities to learn through play at home and in their community. If children growing up today do not experience a substantial amount of play in an early years setting, they will be missing out on many of the character building and life-enhancing experiences many of us took for granted.

Teachers and other practitioners interpret children's need to play in different ways. For some play can simply mean going to the home corner for ten minutes after the child has completed their work. For others it might involve playing a maths board game. It might be what Tina Bruce calls 'free-flow play'. If you consider the various definitions of play given above you will see that since real play involves choice and freedom we must build that into the curriculum. The Curriculum Guidance for the Foundation Stage states that play needs time and space, drawing on Margaret McMillan's philosophy. Ten minutes is not long enough to develop meaningful play.

Research shows that children making a later start to formal schooling generally achieve more academically because their early years experience was meaningful and gave them a more solid foundation for later learning. The Foundation Stage was informed by this research and requires Reception teachers to build on the same play-based curriculum that is well established in the best nursery and pre-school settings.

Some approaches place more value on play than others. Montessori, for example, did not value imaginative play – activity for her was rooted in real life. Steiner, on the other hand, saw play as being of fundamental importance in the early years.

Comment

References
(1) Moyles, J, Adams, S and Musgrove, *A Study of Pedagogical Effectiveness in Early Learning Research Report No 363* (Department for Education and Skills 2002)
(2) Bruce, T *Helping Young Children to Play* (Hodder and Stoughton, 2001)
(3) Lindon, J *Understanding Children's Play* (Nelson Thornes 2001)
(4) Guha, M 'Play in school' in Blenkin, G and Kelly, AV (eds) *Early Childhood Education* (Paul Chapman Publishing 1987)
(5) *The Convention on the Rights of the Child* was adopted by the General Assembly of the United Nations, 20 November 1989

Where to find out more
Helping Young Children to Play Tina Bruce (Hodder and Stoughton 2001)

The Genius of Play S Jenkinson (Hawthorn Press 2001)

International Association for the Child's Right to Play
What is play?
Children are the foundation of the world's future.
Children have played at all times throughout history and in all cultures.
Play, along with the basic needs of nutrition, health, shelter and education is vital to develop the potential of all children.
Play is communication and expression, combining though and action; it gives satisfaction and a feeling of achievement.
Play is instinctive, voluntary and spontaneous.
Play helps children develop physically, mentally, emotionally and socially.
Play is a means of learning to live, not a mere passing of time.

Article 31 of the Convention on the Rights of the Child (7) states that:
Parties recognise the right of the child to rest and leisure, to engage in play and recreational activities appropriate to the age of the child and to participate freely in cultural life and the arts.

Parties shall respect and promote the right of the child to participate fully in cultural and artistic life and shall encourage the provision of appropriate and equal opportunities for cultural, artistic, recreational and leisure activity.

Research into brain development

Emerging evidence about how the young child's brain develops has focused on the importance of providing the best possible learning environment during the early years. Here are some of the findings of current research and their implications for early care and education.

A child's brain begins to develop before they are even born. A developing foetus has its full complement of about 100 billion neurons and the first connections between neurons are already formed. After birth, the process accelerates rapidly with the brain quadrupling in volume by adulthood. This extra volume is made up of new synapses or connections between cells and it is these that are critical for learning and memory.

The neuronal connections are laid down, sculpted and reinforced by regular use. If they are not activated, they decay or are pruned. This process allows those connections which are used frequently more space to grow, explaining young children's obvious 'hunger for experiences' or drive to learn.

Infants play an active role in shaping their own brain. For example, vision is one of the new-born's primary sources of information but the least mature of the senses. During the first six months, the visual cortex, which controls the sending and receiving of visual information, continues to develop until the infant's vision is as clear as an adult's. Babies actively seek out faces in preference to other patterns within half an hour after birth. This speeds up the development of brain connections that process this type of recognition information, so that the baby can quickly distinguish between mum, who represents food, security and comfort - and a stranger.

Babies are particularly attuned to the sound of the human voice. Talking softly and singing to a baby helps develop connections in their brain. The developing brain of young children benefits from the rich and stimulating experiences gained through normal, everyday interactions with caring people.

Based on material written by Dr Jillian Rodd first published in Practical Pre-School magazine (Issue 29).

Development of the brain begins in the foetus and continues until death. However, a timetable controls the brain's natural maturation, making specific physical and mental activities from conception to about 15 months. It ensures that basic survival needs, such as food, shelter, security and safety, are met. It also controls sensory and motor development, which means that young babies' brains require daily opportunities for sensory activation and motor exploration.

From 15 months until about four and a half years of age, the limbic system (see page 79) becomes active, providing the young child with the growing capacity to understand self and others, emotions and language. Now children's brains benefit from regular opportunities for genuine interaction with other children and adults.

From about four to seven years, gestalt hemisphere elaboration makes further expansion of cognitive, language, emotional and physical skills possible. However, it is not until approximately seven to nine years of age, with logic hemisphere elaboration, that the capacity for reading and writing emerges. This suggests that early formal academic learning experiences are inappropriate because children's brains generally do not have the capacity to master such skills until about seven years of age.

Factors that promote brain development

The brain's ability to 'wire' itself depends on a child's exposure to simple learning experiences, such as making sense of faces and patterns and being involved in conversations. Even seemingly mundane experiences, such as staring at toys hanging over a cot or dropping toys and watching them being picked up contribute to this process.

Babies' brains focus their mechanisms for recognising speech at an early age. An infant's repeated exposure to words and vocal interaction clearly helps the brain build neuronal connections that will enable language to be learned later on.

It appears that there are critical periods or windows of opportunity during which the brain is honing particular skills or functions, for example, binocular vision (seeing with both eyes) and language development, specifically the ability to grasp grammatical rules. If the chance to practise a skill is missed during its particular window, the child may be disadvantaged.

Factors that hinder brain development

Considerable evidence suggests that poor pre- and post-natal environments, inadequate nutrition, inappropriate diet, insufficient water and lack of oxygen impede brain growth and reduce the capacity for sensing, learning, thinking and acting.

Young children's brain development appears to be particularly sensitive to stress. Stress raises the level of a steroid hormone that can destroy brain cells and the neural connections needed for later learning. This hormone can trigger hyperactivity, anxiety and impulsive behaviour. It can result

in dissociative behaviour where the child switches off and appears uncommunicative. Chronic stressful experiences, particularly before the age of three when the brain is at its most malleable, can hyper-sensitise children to stressful events which can diminish their ability to concentrate, form relationships and function normally. When children operate in a state of chronic stress, changes to the structure of the brain seem to occur. It is essential that stress be minimised where possible for young children.

Downshifting to a psycho-physiological response occurs when a child is confronted with cognitive tasks that are inappropriate, meaningless, repetitive or present a threat of failure. Environments and teaching strategies that impose undue stress, boredom or fatigue cause some learners to downshift, thereby impeding brain growth and affecting the brain's ability to function at high levels. Early exposure to formal, prescriptive and academic learning experiences can lead to downshifting, thus explaining the disaffection with and disengagement from learning evident in some young children.

Care and attention

The work which has been collated from neuroscientists, researchers and early childhood practitioners indicates that one of the best ways to promote brain development in young children is through responsive care from loving parents and adults. Adult attention is vital because it helps give meaning and context to the developing structures in the brain, thereby grounding learning in social experience.

Stimulating the developing brain's potential does not mean that adults need to resort to specialised or high technology. Many adults provide appropriate, responsive care in their day-to-day interactions with young children. However, a growing body of research indicates that brain growth and development is nurtured by careful attention to all aspects of the child's development - physical, social, emotional, language and cognitive. The infant is born with a pre-disposition to learn and will seek out appropriate stimulation when it is required. Adults need to respond sensitively to children's communications about their learning needs.

Children living in environments that are deprived of stimulation, talk, play and love grow up in unfavourable circumstances. Those who are not played with, sung to, talked to, who receive little tactile stimulation from adults and those who have suffered stressful and traumatic experiences may end up with brains that are measurably smaller or structurally less complex than healthy, loved children. Therefore the real message from brain research has confirmed what many parents and early years professionals have known for years:

- good pre- and post-natal care is vital;
- warm and loving attachments between young children and adults are essential; and
- positive, age appropriate stimulation from birth enhances children's development and learning for a lifetime.

Research into brain development

Many neuroscientists not previously concerned with education, have offered evidence which supports child-centred practices. Ramachandran (1) suggests, for example, that creativity and humour should be part of the curriculum while Susan Greenfield (2) states that 'play is fun with serious consequences'.

Talay-Ongan (3) suggests that the main lessons from brain studies for early childhood practitioners are that:

- Second language learning is easier in the early years;
- Learning is enhanced when the left and right hemispheres are encouraged to work together. This can be done through activities such as music and dance;
- Encouraging visualisation can enhance language;
- There is a better understanding of learning styles;
- Early intervention works best from the first weeks of life;
- Inter-professional work involving neuroscientists, early childhood education practitioners and developmental psychologists is important to a good understanding of learning and development.

Comment

While emerging information about how the young child's brain develops is exciting and illuminating, it is also essential that it is correctly interpreted and translated appropriately into effective early care and educational practices.

We now know that young minds can do more at an earlier age than was previously assumed and that stimulating experiences in natural settings are necessary.

However, prescribing experiences or formal scripts for social or cognitive interactions must be avoided because this results in children's achievements being evaluated too narrowly. Rigid assumptions about what children can, should and will be able to do are not helpful. Unrealistic expectations about the progress of any child, including those with special needs, should be avoided. Narrowing the focus of learning and ignoring the holistic nature of development is detrimental to the well-being of young children.

References
(1) Ramachandran, V S and Blakeslee, S *Phantoms in the Brain* (Fourth Estate 1999)
(2) Greenfield, S *The Human Mind Explained* (Marshall 1996)
(3) Talay-Ongan, *A Typical and Atypical Development in Early Childhood* (British Psychological Society 1999)

Where to find out more
How Brains Think W H Calvin (Weidenfeld and Nicolson 1996)
The Human Brain S Greenfield (Weidenfeld and Nicolson 1997)
How Babies Think Alison Gopnik et al (Weidenfeld and Nicolson 1999) (see page 6)
'Look before you leap: concerns about brain-based products and approaches' S McCormick Davis *Childhood Education* (2000) Winter 100-101
'Examining the emergence of brain development research' M Puckett, C S Marshall and R Davis *Childhood Education* (1999) 76, 1, 8-12
'*What's new?*' P Wolfe National School Improvement Network News Institute of Education, University of London No 19 (2001) Spring 7-8

Howard Gardner's theory of multiple intelligences (1) includes two personal intelligences – interpersonal intelligence and intrapersonal intelligence. The first relates to the ability to interact effectively with others, the second focuses on the ability to reflect on self.

Daniel Goleman borrowed Gardner's use of the word 'intelligence' and developed the concept of emotional intelligence. Emotional intelligence is the capacity to acquire and apply information of an emotional nature, to feel and respond emotionally. It means being able to understand what others are feeling, managing emotions in relation to others and being able to persuade and lead others.

Emotional competencies are skills and attributes such as self-awareness, empathy, impulse control, listening, decision-making and anger management. Emotional literacy is the term used to describe the ability to experience and manage emotions productively.

The power of emotions

Experts in brain development know that emotions are the ignition switch for learning. As we learn more about the brain and how it develops we understand that the emotional mind can over-ride the rational mind.

There are three distinctive parts to the brain: the reptile brain, the limbic system and the neo cortex. The reptilian brain is the most primitive part of the brain. It regulates basic life functions like breathing, monitors motor functions, controls reactions, movement and behaviours that are repetitive, predictable and rarely constructive. The reptilian brain is designed to keep the body running and ensure survival. It is responsible for our 'fight or flight' response when we are faced with danger or negative stress.

As the brain evolved new layers were added. The new layers surrounded the brainstem or reptilian brain like a ring and are called the limbic system. The new neural territory added powerful emotions to the brain's repertoire.

When we are in the grip of anger, full of dread or head over heels in love, the limbic system has us in its grip. This system filters valuable data in and useless data out. It governs our concept of value and truth and is the site of long-term memory and goal setting.

The neo-cortex has evolved most recently and is the seat of thought. It contains the centres that put together and comprehend what the senses perceive. It is responsible for our ability to solve problems, discern relationships and patterns of meaning and it generates meaning from sensory data all of the time.

A small structure in the limbic region of the brain, the amygdala, is the centre of the emotional mind. It scans every incident for trouble. It charges into action without considering the consequences and in moments of crisis or intense passion the emotional brain dominates.

Putting the theory into practice

Emotions play a critical part in teaching and learning. We therefore need to make sure that early years settings are emotionally positive and supportive workplaces for all learners. If learners are exposed to emotionally negative stressors then the reptilian brain dominates and the fight or flight response locks in. No learning takes place. Survival is the key objective. This means that we need to create an environment that:

- is safe and secure;
- is rich in sensory stimuli;

PROFILE

'Emotional intelligence' is a phrase made popular by psychologist and author Daniel Goleman. Goleman defines emotional intelligence as: knowing one's feelings and using them to make good decisions in life; being able to manage moods and control impulses; being motivated and effectively overcoming setbacks in working towards goals.

LINKS

- **Gardner**
- **Psychoanalysis**

Based on material written by Caroline McAdam first published in Practical Pre-School magazine (Issue 28).

Emotional intelligence

- is able to meet the needs of learners;
- is empowering, supporting decision-making and making choices;
- is conducive to positive relationships;
- is free from negative stressors, such as hunger, thirst, threat;
- is emotionally positive, so that feelings are recognised, understood and dealt with effectively;
- fosters achievement and celebrates success;
- is respectful of the difference between learners;
- promotes self-esteem.

It is important not to neglect the emotional life of young children. Feelings, self-awareness, life skills, conflict management and self-esteem are critically important. Emotions direct our behaviour, shape our values and predispose us to choose one course of action over another. They drive us to action, push or pull us away from certain people, objects, actions and ideas. Emotions allow us to defend ourselves in dangerous situations, to love, grieve and protect the things we value.

How children function each day and throughout life is determined by both rational intelligence and emotional intelligence. When the two perform together smoothly and efficiently a child develops in emotional intelligence and intellectual ability.

There is evidence to suggest that those who are emotionally literate are at an advantage in life. Learning involves developing our feelings along with our ability to think and act. How we do in life is determined by our emotional as well as our rational skills.

Most learning involves other people. Working and learning together, discussing our ideas and understandings with others, helps us to develop our personal skills. It also enables us to express a range of emotions, to develop them and to learn to use them effectively.

It is, therefore, important to create a stimulating environment where there are plenty of opportunities to make choices and decisions about the learning that is taking place. Adopting an approach which assumes that young learners are capable of managing themselves, their relationships and their own learning puts the child at the centre of the learning process. Engaging children's minds in investigating aspects of their own experiences and environments helps them to develop a deeper sense of competence and self-worth.

To be most effective, emotional literacy content and processes should be applied consistently across the curriculum. Children need many opportunities for practice. When emotional lessons are repeated over and over, they become positive habits that surface in times of stress. By suggesting relationships and posing the right questions, by being observant and noticing non-verbal signals, adults can help to highlight and deal with emotional aspects of everyday learning. More importantly, they can take moments of personal crisis and turn them into lessons in emotional competence.

Goleman identifies four building blocks for incorporating emotional intelligence in educational settings:

- safety, security, unconditional love and nurturing;
- stimulating environments;
- experimental learning opportunities to engage skills, knowledge and attitudes in a wide variety of real-life tests;
- useful and timely performance feedback.

The role of parents

Family life is a child's first school of emotional learning. Within the family unit they learn how to feel about themselves, how others will react to those feelings, how to think about these feelings and the choices they have in reacting.

Children learn to express themselves, to read others and handle their feelings through modelling or mirroring the significant adults in their lives. The approaches and responses of people around them profoundly influence the children's developing sense of emotions and their impact on daily life. When parents or other significant people respect children, children learn to respect themselves and each other.

Children's confidence and independence depend on their ability to see themselves as reasonably competent and responsible. Adults therefore need to give children real responsibilities through which they can learn.

Comment

Reference
(1) Gardner, H *Frames of Mind* (Fontana 1983)

Where to find out more
Emotional Intelligence Howard Gardner (Bloomsbury 1996)
Working with Emotional Intelligence Daniel Goleman
(Bloomsbury Publishing 1998)
Teaching for Effective Learning (Scottish CCC)
Accelerated Learning in the Classroom A Smith
(Network Educational Press 1996)
Frames of Mind H Gardner (Fontana Press)
The New Leaders (Little Brown Book 2002)